THE ULTIMATE

THE MANY PATHS TO GOD

REALITIES

OF THE

CRUCIFIXION

BOOK FOUR

BY

VERLING CHAKO PRIEST, PHD

Cover layout by author.
Left margin graphic design from Microsoft Works template.

Order this book online at www.trafford.com
or email orders@trafford.com

Most Trafford titles are also available at major online book retailers.

Printed in the United States of America.

ISBN: 978-1-4251-0716-1 (sc)
ISBN: 978-1-4251-9340-9 (e)

Trafford rev. 04/27/2012

www.trafford.com

North America & international
toll-free: 1 888 232 4444 (USA & Canada)
phone: 250 383 6864 ♦ fax: 812 355 4082

DEDICATION

I dedicate this fourth book to God,

Yeshua, and to those Presenters who

graciously came forth to set the records straight.

*"And they entered in, and found not the body of the
Lord Jesus (Luke 24:3)."*

The Ultimate Experience

ACKNOWLEDGMENTS

I must make my first acknowledgment to the Lord Jesus-Sananda. He orchestrated this book from start to finish. I am at a loss for words in order to tell him of my gratitude. He consistently came once a day for three months (except for approximately five times when I had conflicting appointments). As the information of the three realities became more intricately woven, he patiently answered my questions and helped me to move forward with altering my own belief systems. A simple *thank you* does not seem adequate to me for the gifts that he gave me, for not only did he give me this book, but also I was constantly infused with his energy and Light. I give him my heart. Maybe that is all that I need to say.

I thank my daughter, Susan Verling Miller O'Brien, for her willingness and patience in constructing the Table of Contents. When it comes to *Headers* and *Footers* on the computer, my skills do not match what is required, for one mistake and all the pagination is thrown off. That, obviously, is to be my next computer-skill lesson! Therefore, dear Susan, thank you, for you were the key to bringing the framing of this book to its proper conclusion.

I thank Ziranna Dix and Rowena for their helpful insights into the different realities that surrounded the crucifixion. Their validation of what Yeshua and Mariam had been telling me steadied my purpose in writing the book. *Yeshua really wants you to bring this fifth dimensional version into the printed form.* I understand now that he wanted that information anchored into the physical realm. Therefore, I express my deepest appreciation for your help when I was feeling somewhat overwhelmed by all of this.

The Ultimate Experience

Every author needs a proof-reader to catch the typos and delete or add punctuation. I found Heather Clarke. Heather is the founder of the *Arizona Enlightenment Center*. She has a *mental library* that is well stocked with most of the New Age spiritual venues in the Valley. When anyone wants to know who is speaking when and where, he or she asks Heather. Therefore, I am honored that she has the time to take on the project of proofreading this book—no easy task I am afraid! I thank you, dear friend, for all that you do and for coming into my life.

I thank every one of you Readers, for daring to stretch your awareness by reading this book. It may not be an easy journey for most of you, but one we are all sharing.

The Ultimate Experience

PREFACE

I am sitting on my small sofa in the bay window of my bedroom. The tape recorder is on a low table next to this love seat. I sit and wait the Presence of the Masters—these Masters who will be bringing forth that lifetime to experience once again my life as Mariam, Yeshua's cousin and adopted sister.

Ani Williams on her CD softly plays her harp and sings of Mary Magdalene's love for Yeshua (*Magdalene's Gift, Songs to the Beloved*). I hear this in the background setting the tone for this journey. I sit and wait. I think about Yeshua and Mary Magdalene and myself, wondering what that lifetime was like. I feel the familiar emotion start to well up inside of me. I feel the goose bumps. He is near.* He tells me to pick up my tablet and to put what he says in the Preface of our fourth book.

Several months later, the Lord Sananda spiraled his energy down to my crown chakra and instructed me to take it on down into my heart where he told me to embrace him and blend my energy with his. I then was told to take the blended energies on down, through the chakras, and ground our energies into the Earth. *You and I have blended our energies in your heart. All outside energies now come through my energy. We are One, as we always have been. Your Father-Mother God is also watching over you. Therefore, it is with great joy and anticipation that we all look forward to this next step that will come sooner than you have imagined.* Previously, Sananda came in and said, *we have not forgotten our promise to you. We will visit you one of these surprising times in order to bring you into Mariam's extraordinary life. She was every bit as powerful an Essence as was Mary Magdalene and was my dearest friend. (9-2-05)*

It was approximately nine months later that Book FOUR really was started. I was given the title of the book. I was told that *Jesus* would now be referred to as *Yeshua*, his Hebrew name.

The Ultimate Experience

The music I now use to alert Yeshua that I am in place and ready to receive his transmissions is Barbara Streisand's CD, *On Higher Ground*, track #12, AVINU MALKEINU. She sings it beautifully in Hebrew. Yeshua laughingly remarks that it is my *Clarion Call to him and the other Masters.*

I no longer write the transmissions out in longhand, but use my tape recorder, as the words can flow more swiftly, and Yeshua said longhand had become too laborious for both of us. I tried just sitting at the computer, but I could not maintain a high enough vibration and level of concentration to hear the telepathic messages for long periods at a time. I would start *losing them,* as I would put it. Therefore, for now I find that a recorder works best for me.

I thought the book was flowing nicely until they gave me the transmission for the third chapter, *Old Myths Revisited,* with two more along the same theme rapidly following that. Since I reacted in shock, I can well imagine how you Readers will feel. I can say only, *hang in there!* We are pioneers along with Suzanne Ward who was one of the first to write about this new reality of Jesus in April 2000 in her Matthew Book, *Illuminations for a New Era (pgs. 194-200).* God and the Masters want the myths of our belief systems brought to Light. With the Earth raising her vibrations, we must be willing to do our part to help her. Our responsibility is to examine our belief systems having to do with our perceptions of Spirituality. Is there a possibility that many of the important stories in the Bible simply are not true? Yeshua points out the fallacies quite succinctly. Be flexible, Readers—be open to new ideas that will seem at first too outrageous to be true. Many people will be unable to accept these new realities, even though dictated by Yeshua, himself!

By July 26, 2006, our book was over half finished. The Masters changed the title and the original focus of the book from Mariam's story to the *Realities of the Crucifixion.* They have brought forth over sixteen Masters and Ladies, each telling about a segment in his or her past life. That was just the first half of the book! The Masters are incredibly patient, as they frequently reiterate the concepts of three realities that commingled over 2000 years ago.

Humanity is so programmed from well-meaning grandparents, parents, teachers, pastors, and priests to take the written words in our Bibles verbatim. It becomes a lesson in letting go of old beliefs, teachings, spiritual stories, and concepts, for Yeshua tells us that most simply are not true. Each of us needs to keep an open mind and heart and be willing to view the crucifixion through a new lens. This book certainly provides the Reader with that opportunity.

As you read the chapters, you will notice that before and after most chapters there will be italic print. This is to alert you that those words are by Yeshua and me. My words will be in parentheses. However, in the body of the text by the Presenters, italics are again used in place of quotation marks, or to bring to your attention that the Presenter is *smiling* or *laughing.*

I have been asked if the following chapters by the Presenters are set forth verbatim. I give you a qualified *yes.* What I mean by that is that Yeshua has given me permission to edit the material, using my discretion in whatever way that I need. Many times when I spoke through the tape recorder, sentences did not have a clear demarcation. At times, I needed to change or add an adverb, or a grammatical article, or pronoun. I knew what was meant, but the Reader might not. However, the body of the chapter is verbatim.

I have fifteen tapes of ninety minutes each and three of sixty minutes (I think). I did all of the transcribing sitting at my computer. I meticulously typed each word as I heard it. Many times, I would listen to the same sentence repeatedly in order to transcribe it verbatim. Therefore, **I can say reputedly that what you read is what I heard mentally and through my tape recorder—verbatim.** Read on Readers!

CHAKO

The Ultimate Experience

*It was the afternoon of August, 2002 that the Lord Sananda made his presence known by literally stroking my cheek with his finger. While I could not see him, the energy in the room was electrifying. My body trembled in response. He then began speaking to me telepathically. I described that experience in the Preface of my first three books.** However, my proof-Reader said it needed to be said again in this one.

(**Read Books ONE, TWO, & THREE REVISITED 2011, soft cover and e-book ISBN #978-1-4269-765-0 (e). These books had never been self-published before. I just took the accumulated 426 pages and had them spiral bound at Office Max. All of my books can be purchased at either Trafford or Amazon.)

The Ultimate Experience

Table of Contents

The Ultimate Experience

Table of Contents

SECTION 1—Introduction

INTRODUCTION TO THE REALITIES

I AM Yeshua, and Readers, as you open this book and probably flip through the pages, as many of you are wont to do, be aware that there is a great purpose in this book. The purpose is to bring to your attention the different realities that swirled around the crucifixion. In your Bible, it is presented as only one reality—the crucifixion. However, what we want to light up for you is that there were different realities in play. The most prevalent reality, odd as it may seem, was not the actual **real** play. It was staged. **It was a staged play by me as Jesus and by God**. The players in the play were my Disciples, the twelve Apostles, the Roman government and the Sanhedrin—those priests and rabbis who felt that only they had the interpretation of the Laws, for they allowed no leeway. No one else was to go beyond the boundaries that the Sanhedrin had put out. You could think of it as a box. You could not go outside of the box.

Of course, I was a thorn in their side. I was becoming too popular, for the people wished to hear about God in ways that they had never heard. They wanted to know about this Kingdom of Heaven. They had never heard that. They wanted to know that God, while He could be a forceful God, could be gentle, loving, and caring of them. He loved them. He had guided them out of Egypt. He had guided them throughout the long years in the desert, as they wandered and raised their vibratory rate enough so that they could enter the land of milk and honey—what has become known as Israel. He led them.

However, they were always afraid of Him. They had been taught to fear Him, that he was an awesome, fearsome God. He could be, but the message I was bringing to them was Love; they were loved. To those of you who are not Fundamentalist Christians, it may seem as if I am speaking in those Christian terms. I am not. It is a Universal language of Love. He loves you. God, the Father, loves you. The people were hungry to hear this.

The Ultimate Experience
INTRODUCTION TO THE REALITIES

There were so many edicts from the old time religion that they were hungry for something else.

Of course, when I say the *people*, there were the Gentiles and the Jews. The Jews were not happy with my message, while the Gentiles were hungry for it. Keep in your minds, Readers, the difficulty during that ancient era of over 2000 years ago. People did not have the consciousness that you do now. They did not have the mentality of awareness that you do now. You see, your awareness and your consciousness have been able to leap in tremendous strides because of the inventions that you have. You have the television; you have radio; you have printing presses. None of this was manifested yet 2000 years ago. Therefore, the people were slower in their evolution to change their ways. However, in this generation, people are apt to embrace too much of what they read and see on TV and think of it as being real.

That brings me back to the different realities. In one sense, the crucifixion was real to people in that lower dimension—what we will call the *third dimension*. Some were actually still in the second dimension, those lower energy centers. That was the mentality of the people—to want to take revenge. In their negative righteousness, they would enflame a crowd. They would cater to the mob mentality. Since they did not have guns then, they would bend down and pick up anything that would fit in their hand and throw it. That is where the stoning came from. If you carried bow and arrows, it would be an arrow of some kind, or a spear.

However, in this generation, people carry guns and can shoot each other. Back in my day when they did not have guns, they stoned each other. Usually after joining a mob mentality, they would then stone you. The Apostle Matthew was stoned to death. It is not a pleasant death unless you were lucky enough to have the first stone hit you in the temple and kill you. Usually, it was a painful death—very painful.

Therefore, there was this mentality, this lower-dimensional mentality, a group mind; and if you were in that mentality, you would be in that particular dimension. In that dimension, you would draw to you thought forms; you would create thought forms. The thought forms said *we must crucify him for causing so much trouble and going against the Laws.* Keep in mind I too was a Jew and in my mind I was merely putting in a new interpretation to a Law. We have said before about the fact that I interpreted more loosely the Law about doing no labor on the Sabbath.

I have spoken about this before, for that Law was put into a box and you could not get it out. People went overboard about that. That Law was supposed to be a Law of rest. You worked hard all week; now rest and pray to God and think of God. Our Sabbath was on a Saturday. The Christians have made their Sabbath on a Sunday. I wonder what they would have thought about my channeling, Jesus-Yeshua channeling on a Sunday (*smile*).

Many times, I have come to this channel and have spoken to her on a Sunday. She goes to church occasionally. I have told her there are many people in church every week who do not carry the depth of spirituality that she has. She is precious to me, and we have blended our energies so that I come to her whenever I wish and she may do the same with me. We have a contract that we can communicate with each other whenever we wish. Therefore, I have come to her on her Christian Sundays (*smile*). I have come to her on the Hebrew Saturdays. If you can, just let go of those belief systems that are strangling you. Let them go. Be open to new ideas.

Can you be open to the fact that there may have been other realities around the crucifixion? **Can you be open to the fact that maybe I was not crucified?** Oh-oh, I think I may have just lost some of you! Of course, I am smiling with you, but the realities, you see, were not always what you thought them to be. The mentality of the people brought a crucifixion into being. They did not know about thought forms, about energies of that nature. They did not know they could bring to them what they had thought in vengeance.

The Ultimate Experience
INTRODUCTION TO THE REALITIES

They thought about crucifying me. Therefore, they made that happen in that dimension. However, was it real? They thought so. Was I killed? No, but they thought so. Was it me on the cross? Hmm, I think I will let you ponder on that for a while, Readers, for the secret is in the different chapters that follow this Introduction.

Let us talk about another dimension, for the reality of the cross was in the lower third. Let us talk about the higher dimension, like the higher fifth and into the sixth dimensions. Do you think that ugliness, that revengeful heart energy can be manifested in that higher fifth dimension? We are talking about vibrations. A vengeful person is in such a low vibration. In that higher fifth dimension, the energy of lower dimensions cannot be manifested, for the vibration at the higher fifth is very high, very fast, very pure, and a Love energy. There are higher and higher dimensions from that even. However, if you are in the fifth dimension...let us put it this way: Go back in history 2000 years ago, but stay in the fifth dimension. What would you see? Would you see wars with people fighting and killing each other? No, for that energy, those thought forms, could not exist in the fifth dimension. Consequently, would that crucifixion scene have happened in the fifth dimension? No, it could not exist. It simply could not exist.

I know this is confusing to people. Why do you think we wrote a whole book on it *(laughingly)*? This channel even was struggling with these concepts. There is another reality. Do I dare mention it *(smile)*? I think I will let you find that one by reading the book. Therefore, we have these three realities commingling. One of them in the fifth dimension did not happen. One of them in the next reality did happen because of the mob mentality and the human mass consciousness of that time. You will find out about the third reality when you read the book. There are three realities, Readers, each holding a different energy vibration—each holding a different consciousness.

The Ultimate Experience
INTRODUCTION TO THE REALITIES

There have been authors, Readers, who wrote about the crucifixion. In our first three books, we did also, *carrying on the fable*, as I put it. However, it was too soon, you see, to tell you. The first three books had to be written before this fourth one could come forth. The first three are no longer in print as manuscripts.* It will take a great deal of time to edit them. The author simply may not have time for such an undertaking. On the other hand, she may be selective and just take out the chapters that spoke on various issues and put them all under one heading. That is a possibility also.

Therefore, Readers, this book will awaken you to new ideas. This book will give you a jolt. It will be your choice whether you wish to accept it or reject it. Remember, you have your free will. It always is your choice as to whether you wish to change or not. Those who change go forward. Those who do not change tread water a while. They may never change; or they may finally go forward. It is always your choice and always at your own pace of consciousness—taking those steps on your path.

We sincerely hope—I, Yeshua, and the other players in the book—that you take in our words and know that we speak Truth. One statement that I can make is that your life is real to you, but is everything else real around you? Is your television real? The mechanics of it are, but are the pictures that come forth real? Most likely they are not. Is your media real? The mechanics are, but what they put forth for you to read—is it real or is it an illusion? They print only what they are allowed to print, which many times can be the lies from your government.

It is an interesting fact that every president elected tells the truth when he wishes to and then tells the lie if it makes his situation look better in the eyes of the public. Governments do not tell the whole truth to the people. America has democracy, but it is not a true democracy in which one can trust the leaders, for your government is ruled by the powerful that have a long legacy of being in power. It has gone on for centuries. It is time now for power to release its hold on people. It is time now for people to be able to hear the Truth. Probably this government more than the others from the past is to be trusted less.

Remember what you have been told. The dark must rise in order to be transmuted by the Light. Therefore, if your government has gone dark it must come to the forefront, so that it can be transmuted to the Light. Think of cream rising to the top of a bottle. The cream must be poured off—skimmed off—so that only the healthy part is left. Your government is in a precarious situation, and the political party that is in control in 2006 is fighting for its life. Will it be voted into power still? It is doubtful, for it must change. The dark rises so that the Light can transmute it. Therefore, it must change.

Now how, Readers, does a change come about? It comes by the willingness to be open to hear new ideas. That is what has brought your government and its political party down, for they—the president and all who surround him—have refused to let anyone else's ideas in—only the power from the past. Only the power is allowed. That has brought the government down.

Do you see why I have brought this up? We are talking about realities. Do you see why there was a crucifixion? Crucifixion has become a metaphor. One could say that the people are rising up and the Republican Party of this present government is going to be crucified.** That is the mentality of the people right now. They are fed up with the war that was not necessary. It simply was self-serving for the higher political figures. It was greed. They could have cared less about bringing democracy to Iraq. They have done nothing but destroy that country and would destroy other countries if they were allowed. They overturned a huge rock that unleashed all manner of darkness. (**The USA government of 2006*)

This is what happened during the crucifixion. People could not hear Truth. They were afraid they might lose their positions of power. They were afraid. Therefore, that mentality took the man, Jesus, and crucified him—that reality. However, did that reality happen in the fifth dimension? No, there was no crucifixion. If

7

that crucifixion happened in that lower third dimension, **was Jesus actually crucified? No, he was not!** You must read further, Readers. I have tweaked your curiosity; I hope. Read further.

You will find that we have brought forth many great Souls to the point that this author even was questioning, for she was channeling half of the twelve Apostles and she could not believe it (*laughingly*). We had a method to our madness; we had a method (*still laughing*), for you see, each Apostle came forth for a reason. That reason was to set the record straight. They were able at last to refute what was said about them. It was quite amazing. My beloved Mary Magdalene was never what you would call a *fallen woman*. She was not stoned. She was not part of any of that Biblical-type history. She was my wife and the love of my life. I will put that right up front, in case you do not know it yet—we were married and we had children.

Therefore, that was one myth. As **Peter** said, we were popping balloons, and he popped a balloon when he said that **he never denied me three times**. He wanted that erased. He did not want you to think that every time you heard a cock crow you would think of his denying me. He really was upset with that one (*laughingly*). He did not want that to carry forth (*laughter*).

Now, let me see what another one is. Oh, Judas, **my dear friend, Judas, did not betray me**—ever—oh, the different myths that have gone on. He never betrayed me. Therefore, each one tells his or her story, the purpose being to give you a new reality, so you can let all of those beliefs go—the stories that you were told by your Sunday school teachers. Let them go. Just think of them as stories, not real, not true, but stories, as a myth. **Put this whole crucifixion in your mind as a myth**. Someday the Bible will be rewritten. Whether it will be by King James, my brother, or not, I do not know. It must be rewritten, for there always needs to be a Book that people can go to, read the words, and receive the energy from the words and the energy of God—and the solace and caring that He gives you. There need to be Bibles for people.

8

The Ultimate Experience
INTRODUCTION TO THE REALITIES

They are called differently by the different religions—the Torah for the Hebrews. They are all words from God.

Therefore, my dear friends, I hope you will continue reading. I hope this Introduction has not turned you away from furthering your own consciousness. Trust in your Higher Self. Trust in your heart and know that we are giving you Truth this day. I now will step back and let another come forth. This Introduction will have several of the cast members speaking. When I say *cast*, I mean the members of our dramatic play. I am forever yours—yours in heart and Spirit. I bless you, **I am Yeshua.**

Hello to our dear Readers, **I AM Mother Mary.** I come to say a few words for the Introduction of our book. You have heard from my son concerning the words we have written and concerning the realities that swirled around the crucifixion. Much has been written about me—the speculations as to what I did, what I said, my purported virgin birth of our son—oh, Readers, open your minds; open your minds.

In the book, our Father makes a good point about the whole virgin birth of Emanuel, so I will jump to his age of thirty-three when humanity forced him onto the cross. Now Yeshua has just told you that there were different realities swirling around. With humanity's consciousness, their thought forms, their energies, their ways of approaching life, they brought this crucifixion onto themselves. Was it real? Ah, here lies an interesting question, for parts of it were real and parts not real. How is that for a quizzer to give you the incentive to read on? It is a puzzle, is it not?

He was called before the Sanhedrin and the Roman government. That was true. He was warned in a fierce way and they did whip him, but not in the gory way that was shown in your movie by Mel Gibson in the *Passion of the Christ*. That did not happen. You must have many questions I would think, having read the part that Yeshua has spoken just now. Yet there are those of you who have such closed minds that you will not believe any other way. You are what we would term a *Fundamentalist,* I believe, who only embraces the words in the Bible whether they are correct or not. I tell you, Readers, that many of the sayings, words, and stories simply are not true. They are not true!

They had Mother Mary, Mary Magdalene, and others not mentioned including this channel as Mariam who was very much a part of my family, huddling at the foot of his cross. That is not true. The story has us going to the tomb after the crucifixion. That is not true. The story has the stone at the mouth of the tomb rolled back. That is not true. Did Yeshua stand and greet us? Yes, he did. He greeted us in real form. Did he carry the nail scars on his wrists and feet? No, he did not, for that was not true.

Now this is where people become perplexed. However, keep in mind about the different realities. There was the reality of a crucifixion brought upon by the peoples' lower thought forms. The evil ones wanted to crucify him. Nevertheless, this will be a puzzler for you until you have read the book and understand. At the conclusion, I will make another statement. Know that you will be delving into material of which you may never have thought—perhaps never allowed yourself these thoughts, for it can be outrageously different from anything that you have ever known. There will be many challenges, dear Readers, many opportunities for you to let go of your old beliefs and to only hear a new reality and a new Truth. I urge you to be open. I urge you to allow these new seeds of information to germinate. By reading this chapter, we have planted those seeds for you. Let them germinate. Do not kill them by refusing to go further. Let them germinate. Dare to take that next step. I urge you when you read this book to read it from cover to cover. Do not jump around because each chapter leads you to another reality—will lead you gently to it page-by-page, step-by-step. Please do not read it all in one sitting. Take at least two days if you can, for it is a page-turner, as the saying goes.

Will this book ever be published in hardbound? It is doubtful, for it is before its time.* The manuscripts will be available to anyone who wishes to buy one. It will spread by word of mouth just as the others did. It will go forth in a wider range than the others did. However, it is going only to those who are willing to open their minds, or who already have opened minds. If your mind is closed, where you can think only of what you are taught or read, then you will have lost the opportunity to go forward in your own consciousness. (*The book was published 2006!*)

I urge you to read this book and ponder its contents. Let it germinate. Let it evolve in your own consciousness. Let it be a catalyst to bring changes to you. You will be surprised if you open yourself to these new ideas; you will be surprised how fast they can bring you forward. It will be like a release from bondage from old ways of thinking. Release your bondage, my dear children. Call upon me if you need help. I am always with you—only a thought away. With that, I give you my blessings. **I am Mother Mary**.

Yeshua comments: *Now let us bring forth Mariam. You see it is important that you acknowledge who Mariam was. She was my sister and I wish to have her acknowledged as so in this book.*

I AM Mariam. For those of you Readers who may not know who I am, I am the adopted cousin who became a sister to Yeshua. My mother Rebekah had died of leprosy. My father in his grief went back to the Qumran area, and I felt quite alone in my grief. Therefore, my destiny was now with the Holy Family. They took me in whole-heartedly. It took me a while to adjust, but there was a rapport, and always had been a rapport with Yeshua and me. We bonded as brother and sister.

Later when Yeshua left around the age of twelve or thirteen and went on his travels—I believe it is noted to be *the lost years of Jesus*—I became best friends with Mary Magdalene. When we were at Mount Carmel, we had many talks and discussions, and usually it ended up being about Yeshua (*chuckle*). We were both **in** love with him, for my sisterly love verged on the hope I would marry him someday. However, that was not to be. That was not my destiny. That was Mary Magdalene's destiny. It was our pre-birth agreement. Therefore, I accepted that. I soon found love with Nathaniel who was a handsome man and an endearing husband. We had a precious son, Benjamin. Therefore, the first two chapters of this book are about the time that I was with Yeshua as a close brother and sister. I then tell of my family with Benjamin and Yeshua coming to visit us.

This book is about the crucifixion, the three different realities that surrounded it. At first we thought the book would be more focused on the lifetime I had with Yeshua. However, it soon became obvious that the book needed to be about the crucifixion. There is such controversy about this. We decided to keep the first two chapters and **then** jump right in. We wanted to lead you Readers in gently and still give a bit of the personal history when Yeshua was in his youth. Then later we would bring forth the concept of the different realities, which may be a bit of a shaking for you if you have not heard about those realities. It is sort of a *wake-up call*.

I was part of those realities. I was one of Yeshua's Disciples, although I was never named as such. The women were not allowed that title, I guess, but we followed him. Since Mary Magdalene was married by then to Yeshua, my husband, Nathaniel, accompanied me many times, as did my son Benjamin. During those times that they did not, Mary Magdalene and I, as best friends and confidants, walked the land together. Yeshua treated us women with respect. Of course he would with Mary, for she was his wife, but there were other women who came with us—the Disciples' wives plus others.

History has it where prostitutes would follow bands of men that wandered the countryside or followed the armies. However, I assure you (*chuckle*) there were no prostitutes following our band of people! Most the women who came with us were married. Sometimes a woman would bring along someone to help her— what you might call a *serving girl*. One could say there were many chores on the trip. We women did our woman-duties in that patriarchal society. We provided the water for people to bathe in. We helped prepare the meals at places that were given us to do so. Other times food was given to us.

Mary and I many times were put into the position of teaching the Disciples and the Apostles. By that I mean we explained some of Yeshua's parables. While he put them in very simple form, Aramaic for the common people, there was still a great deal of interpretation. An Aramaic word could have different meanings. Therefore, we helped with the meaning of his stories, for **we** knew. Some of the men were simple men. They were not educated or highly educated and did not always know the meaning of what was said. Not all of them took kindly to our teaching. We did not push it. We let them get used to us. Not everyone knew each other. Consequently, it was like other groups. You get to know each other before you started putting your ideas into the mix. However, in the end they came to trust what we had to say. They came to trust that we were not trying to usurp any of their positions. They became our extended family.

We were all together approximately three years before the Romans got too nasty and Yeshua had some decisions to make, for his life was getting to the point where he was in danger. This book, Readers, will shock many of you, especially if you have not been that informed with New Age thought. (*Laughingly)* Let us put it this way. If you read the Da Vinci Code, enjoyed it, and were not upset with it, then this book may be just fine for you. However, if you are in the group that thought of the Da Vinci Code as blasphemous, or sacrilegious, anything of that nature and just condemned its author, then maybe this book will not be for you either. It certainly does not agree with the Bible. This book may never be published, since it is so controversial. However, it seems to be a fact that when something is of a controversial nature, it has a way of getting around. People want to hear about it. They want to read it for themselves and then make up their mind. Give it to another person and the word will spread. For now, it will remain in manuscript form. We shall see, for when you talk about *possibilities and probabilities,* this book being published is still in the *possibility* range. It has not made it to the *probability* category yet. Who knows? If humanity changes its outlook and accepts new ideas, then the category could change also. I can tell you this, Readers, much that the Bibles tell is not very true. We have suggested putting many of those stories into mythology, similar to Greek mythology, for so many of the stories are not true. However, there will be other books by this author and through this author.

One of the first things that Fundamentalist Christians always want to know is whether you have read the Word, meaning the words written in the Bible. There is energy in those words. However, they cannot be taken verbatim. It is said that the Apostles wrote this and that, but after the church fathers got through with it, it is doubtful what they have written. Therefore, we do not take the Bible verbatim. Nevertheless, what you can do is know that the characters of that magnificent play were real. I have heard one person say to this author *I don't even know if Jesus existed.* We can say to that *oh yes he did, he is very much real. He was then and is still today!*

Do you know, Readers, that when Yeshua sets up this book or any book he overshadows the channel so that literally any Being who comes forth to the mental body to transmit literally comes through his energy. This is in order to protect her. It keeps the Beings that pretend they are masters—the wanna-be—away from her. Therefore, when you read what these different great Souls have said, you can believe it. *Is that really Plato, the Philosopher?* Yes, it is. *Is that really Saint James, the one who became King James?* Yes, it is. Each Contributor in this book comes through Yeshua. You can think of it in terms of a gate and he is standing at the gate. *Do you have the password?* Therefore, you can trust that all of the Beings that have contributed to this book are real and have come through Yeshua. If you trust him, then you can trust the book.

The Ultimate Experience
INTRODUCTION TO THE REALITIES

There has been much said about the relationship between Mary Magdalene and Yeshua. Many, many people refuse to believe that they were married. They were! If people got that far, they now refuse to believe that the Holy Couple had children. They did! If they got that far, they further refuse to believe that they had more children than just one. They did! Some of the New Agers know about a daughter named Sarah, but they do not know about the sons. He had sons and daughters. Some were born in India and some were born in France—so many stories. It is interesting that this channel's youngest daughter is named Sara, not that there is any connection, but just a bit of coincidence perhaps.

I have nothing more that I feel would be helpful for you in this *Introduction*, so I will say *adieu* for now and meet you again in the first chapter. Blessings to all of you, I am Mariam, the sister to Yeshua and an aspect of this channel. Oh, did I forget to tell you that? Hmm, I did, on purpose (*smile*). 'Til later, **I am Mariam.**

I AM Father Joseph, the father of my magnificent son who you know as Yeshua, and for the Introduction for this book, I wish to make some comments on some of the myths that surround the conception of my son. It has been written so many times of Mother Mary's virgin birth and conception. That is one reality, but the Truth is, dear Readers, that Mary was a virgin of course and we married. You see that is where the interpretation got off track. The scribes said we did not marry and she was impregnated by an angel and then Jesus was born. That is not accurate. We married and in that beautiful act, we consummated that marriage and she became pregnant with my seed. It was still an Immaculate Conception, for we kept our energies at the highest form of consciousness. No lust entered into our union, so in that way, it was immaculate, a pure conception.

I carried the Light codes in my seed, as Mary carried the Light codes in her womb. Therefore, when we had the grand union, the Light codes exploded and the result was our magnificent son, Yeshua. There were many Beings helping the union that day.

The Ultimate Experience
INTRODUCTION TO THE REALITIES

You may not know this but over one hundred Beings surrounded us in the etheric realm. They were maintaining the energies and bringing balance to the bodies, all done through the etheric bodies. The two physical bodies were in their passion, but the angels and Beings of the highest form were energizing and helping on the etheric so that the conception would take place.

I imagine that some of you Readers are aghast at this. *Do you mean everybody is watching?* I am afraid so. (*Smile*) However, in the heat of your passion, you could probably care less. (*Laughingly*) Even in humanity when conception is to take place, there are Beings that surround you and help you—maybe eight or ten, your guides, or maybe your teachers. Therefore, everybody has a hand in this magnificent creation.

There is not a great deal written about me in the Bible, which is probably just as well, for it would not be that accurate anyway, except yes, I was a carpenter—an artisan of fine woods. That was true. It is written that I died while Yeshua was away. Well, the reality is he was away, but I died in the Himalayas. The scribes had not written that, for how could they write that when they would not acknowledge that I was there? I had gone there for spiritual work. I also knew I would make my Ascension from there. Consequently, I chose the highest part of the world, we could say, from which to ascend. Therefore, you have another reality in which to ponder. Was it the one written in the Bible? Did I die in Israel? No, that is not Truth. I traveled. I was a deeply spiritual man, you see. I was an Essene, and we had been taught about Initiations and Ascensions. I carried that information and I knew it. I had that awareness. Therefore, I went to the Himalayas to study more and from there to make my ascension.

Keep in mind, Readers, that when you read of these different things happening, you may say to yourself *gosh, why did he do that? Why did he go there?* Keep in mind you have set up your life before you were born. I knew I was to go there and I did—to the Himalayas. I went there for a purpose. I wanted more wisdom on certain teachings. Where was I going to get that wisdom?

Certainly not in the density where I was at that time in that land of Israel. The only great Teacher roaming that country at the time was my son! That is why he was sent there. He was one of the four pillars. He was sent there by God.

This would drive the Sanhedrin and priests to distraction, for Yeshua would talk freely about his Father having sent him there. The Rabbis would think that was blasphemous. It was not in their thinking, in their perceptions that God would send you somewhere. They were so busy creating fear in people, having people fear this revengeful God. It was not Truth that they were teaching. Then here comes a man, a young one, who seemed to have no reservations about what he was saying whatsoever. As his brother said to him, *how do you do that? How do you get the guts for that? (Smile)* He was so in touch with who he was. He was on a Higher Soul level than even he knew. Before he matured, it would perplex him as to why others did not know. He just knew. To use a New Age phrase, he just *brought it all in with him.* Oh how I loved that son of mine. However, I too knew my purpose and knew what I had come in to do. That was the true reality. I knew the purpose, as did Mary. We knew more than most people realized.

It is so difficult now in your modern times to realize the different realties that were involved. Today there are also different realities commingled. That is why you hear all the time that life is an illusion—different realities commingling. I think that is all I need to say for this *Introduction* chapter. The Father will be speaking also, for He has a message for you Readers that He wishes to give to you. Therefore, I will close for now and meet you again further on in the book. **I AM Father Joseph.**

Well, dear Readers, **I AM your God, your Father-Mother God**. I am delighted to come again. We changed the book somewhat, so some of us had to come back to reiterate what we had said before.

One of the points I wish to address is this myth about the *Immaculate Conception*—such a loaded term that is. It has different interpretations. *Immaculate* of course means something totally clean and totally pure. *Conception* means the impregnation during the union of a man and woman. However, I wish to give you another perspective. An *Immaculate Conception* can be on an energy, vibratory, frequency level, a harmonic level, where the energies are high and pure and above the common act. The conception of Yeshua was in the highest act there can be.

However, people still believe that Joseph and Mary did not have a physical union—that it all was ethereal, that an angel impregnated her. That is a beautiful story—another reality that people perpetuate to this day! **Moreover, a beautiful myth, for it did not happen.** As you know, I created man and woman. I created that closeness, how they would propagate their species. It is My creation that a man and a woman would come together in passion and bliss and that his seed would pass into the woman. She would receive it in joy and love. That is what happened. That is the Truth of it.

Some of your Fundamentalists, and maybe others, seem to think that Yeshua's conception ought not to be the normal way. *I must raise his conception above this sinful act and have an angel plant the seed.* That is not logical. Why would I raise him above all My other children? If I developed the process of creating life for all humans, why would I even consider it not being appropriate for Yeshua? That way of making love and then impregnating a woman is blissful. It is perfect in every way when it is done correctly with love and in the highest energies of Light, as in the union of Mary and Joseph.

When I and Yeshua, Mary, Joseph, and others of the Holy Family came together before anyone was born, We worked out the lessons to be learned—what was to be accomplished, and how it was to be accomplished. There was great planning involved. One does not just pop into a life and wait for it to tell you how it is going to proceed. You orchestrate it. It is your free will and your plan and your life. If your life says you are going to have babies with a certain man, then that is what happens. You have planned this. You came up with a magnificent plan to help humanity—to help humanity to change its ways. Did it work? I am sad to say that in the free will of people, they distorted the play.

Some people frown on psychic phenomenon—going to a *psychic* or *seer* for information. They frown on that and frown on astrology. They say *well, if your life is planned, then fate is. Fate* enters in when you take free will into consideration. Free will can change your fate. Sometimes people are so caught up in their bodies and their free will takes over. They forget their purpose. They forget why they came. Their souls come to Earth and forget more and more, for their free will starts to distort the original plan.

This is what happened with Christianity. The church fathers distorted the original teachings and the original plan. Now lest you forget, everyone, all of humanity is My child. I love each of you, each of you equally. Therefore, if a church father has distorted what was planned, I still love him. He is my child. That is what makes it interesting for Me to watch My creations (*smile*), for they are always surprising Me in what they do.

Therefore, Readers, in this book know that We (and I AM a part of this book) are breaking up your myths. Each chapter will shock you a little, perhaps. Then you sit with that. Maybe what I have just said about Mary and Joseph conceiving Yeshua will have shocked you. Just sit with that. **It was not a virgin birth. It was not an Immaculate Conception in the physical sense—on an energy level it was.** As you get deeper into the book, just keep in mind what is real and what is not real. What is the reality interwoven with another reality? Then you separate them in your mind. Can you let that which is not real go? Can you let those beliefs go?

I do watch over you. I do watch what you are doing and I do love you. Enjoy this book, for it has much to teach you. It is written in a simple way—the way that Emanuel prefers—simple teachings, reiterated many times so that when you close the book on the last page, your beliefs will no longer be the same. The transmutation will have started—the change will have occurred. For Me, that is a very happy thought and I hope you think so too. With that, My children, I bless you. **I AM your Mother-Father God.** *

*People question on whether one can channel God, the Father. My first experience was when Jesus brought Him forth for my first book, which carries the same title as this one. God made one of the closing statements. I will repeat some of that here.

I send the world My Energies of love, peace, hope, and compassion. It breaks My heart to observe so much despair, when in actuality there ought to be none! My Kingdom is open for all to enter. He or she does not have to be Muslim, Jew, Buddhist, or Christian. You are all My children in your beautiful shades of colors, with your unique looks, actions, and cultures. What a glorious melting pot you are, My children.

He comments further and then closes with *I AM your Father, who is not on high and inaccessible, but in your hearts and throughout this beautiful planet, Earth. Part of My Plan is for Heaven to be on Earth—that there is such a blending that there is no more separation.*

I bid you good day and give all of you My Eternal Blessings!

SECTION 2—The Presenters

THE BUG FORT

I AM Mariam, back once again. We have finished the Introduction chapter. Let us now proceed, for we can name the next chapter later on when you get the flavor of it.

I was a happy child. I took great joy in observing Nature. I felt protected as if nothing would rattle my world. However, it was with great sorrow when I beheld my dying mother—leprosy. We were at Mount Carmel at that time with the Essenes. My grandmother, Anna, and the body of healers tried their best to heal my mother, but to no avail.

However, as many of you know, when it is time for a soul to make that transition, nothing will heal the body. It was Rebekah's time. How painful that is for the young daughter who is left behind. Nothing could console me. My father in his own grief left me in the care of the Essenes. Eventually, I was adopted into the family of Mary and Joseph, Yeshua and his brothers and sister. Little did I know at that time that that was God's plan and my soul's agreement? In fact, it was every soul's agreement that was involved. For a young child, of approximately nine years or so, it was a very difficult time indeed.

Now this book is for the edification of you Readers. It is to provide you with little bits and pieces showing the normalcy of our family. People have put our family, known as the Holy Family, on a pedestal. However, at that time, we did not know we were special. We were just living our life as people do now. We were all doing the best that we could.

It was during that first year while I was being integrated into that beautiful family, that I began to realize my good fortune. So much now a-days is talked about the dysfunctional family and all the abuse that happens in those families—but not in my family! We were very happy, very happy. They did everything, or as the saying goes, *they bent over backwards* to bring me into their hearts, which they did and I returned their love.

One day Yeshua and I were playing as young people do. We felt totally relaxed with each other. There was no boy-girl stuff—just brother and sister who liked each other and loved each other. However, I must admit my love had a rather girlish component to it in that I hoped that some day we would marry. However, I have spoken about that to you before. It was not to be. Anyway, one day we were sitting among the trees. Actually, we were lying down, not really close, but our heads were almost touching. We were sprawled out in a V shape. We would cross our knees and dangle our feet as young bodies do. Yeshua was taller than I was, although we were about the same age. We had a little contest. The contest was how many bugs could be found, for if you looked closely there would be a little bug here and another one there. None of them would harm you. Each bug was doing its bug-thing. We made a little fort for bugs and put some leaves in there and then we went bug hunting.

As we found this little bug or that little bug, we let it crawl up on a stick or a leaf and we took it to the bug fort (*smile*). We never thought that they would not like each other. To us a bug was a bug. With our heads together it was with great delight that we watched the bugs in our little bug fort. When we grew tired of that, we picked up the sticks and dismantled the fort so that the bugs could go about their business. I am giving you this little example to show you that we were just normal kids playing with anything that we could lay our hands on, using our imaginations, and watching Nature.

Sometimes we would laugh and compare each other to the bugs that we had captured in the bug fort. One of us would say, *oh, you are just like that little bug that always hides under a leaf.* The other one would say, *oh, you are just like that little bug that tries to fly away.* We compared ourselves with the little bugs of Nature. That became a pattern for, as we got older we then would say we were caterpillars in a chrysalis, and I was the butterfly that moved and flew about. He was the caterpillar that methodically went about eating and filling himself with knowledge. It was quite amazing. No one would suspect now that we compared ourselves with little bugs from Nature. However, you see, dear Readers, we were just children. We did not stay serious very long and we learned how to play with whatever was at hand. In this case, it was little bugs. We even picked little wildflowers and brought them to our bug fort, so the little bugs could see beauty also. We never kept them encaged for very long. It was a source of amusement and a real interest for us to watch these tiny little creatures of Nature.

At another time, we lay on our backs and we watched the clouds. We imagined that this cloud was a wooly sheep. How many sheep could you see in the sky? We let our imaginations, as the saying goes, *go wild* while we watched the sheep in the sky. That was the type of playing that we did. At that age, we were still at Mount Carmel. We had our lessons to learn and our tasks where everybody worked. There still was a demarcation between tasks for females and tasks for men, but probably less so than in other places. Women had the changing of linens, the washing and drying, remaking of beds, harvesting, washing and chopping the vegetables, and cooking the meals. Women did all of that. Men also worked the gardens, harvested them, and studied.

One day when it was our rest period and we could do what we wished, Yeshua and I took a walk where there were beautiful areas with trees. We then sat down and started telling each other what we thought our life would be. Yeshua knew that he had a mission. He was getting more insight daily. I knew I was to help him in some way. I had no idea how, for we did not know about Disciples then. We both expressed that we knew we were to be together in some way, but we did not know how or the purpose. Not knowing the purpose added some confusion, but then we just decided to let our path unfold all in God's timing. We really knew that. One must wait for God's timing. We spoke freely of God, for it was not in a religious setting. We spoke of Him as one would of a Father who we knew was watching us and planning our future. It was very simple. There were not any religious overtones at all. Yeshua would express to me, *I know I am here for a reason, but I do not know what it is.* Then I would echo, *I know that I am here for a reason also, and I believe that my reason is part of yours in some way.* Then he would agree and nod his head, *yes, I feel that too.* Then we would make some silly remark and double over in laughter. We brought much humor into our conversations. We would dip our toe into the depth of something and then take it out with a laugh and do something else. We did not tarry in that deeper meaning very long; for we knew that we really did not have the answers. However, we both felt it.

Now dear ones, I wish to address a more serious subject. As we grew in years and Yeshua grew in stature, there came a time when Yeshua in the Hebrew sense had reached adulthood, a man. His Uncle Joseph of Arimethea took him on quite a long journey that would cover many countries and keep him from my sight for years. Again, I was inconsolable, for by then he was the love of my life. He was my confidant, companion, and the joy in my life.

Now he was leaving me. I realized that he had his calling to travel. I knew it was God's will, but the human part of me anguished, just anguished. It brought up all the grief and separation that I had with my mother's death. However, at the same time it brought me to a realization that I was not to marry Yeshua ben Joseph. I was to get on with my life. In the meantime I did have a dear friend, Mary Magdalene. We talked incessantly about Yeshua, as young girls will.

Mary Magdalene was a beautiful woman with deep auburn red hair. So much has been written about her that is not true, but that is her story. Maybe she will write about it someday. I only wish to say that my relationship with Mary Magdalene grew with a fastness or a bonding, if you wish, that was unbreakable. I trusted her integrity and her honesty, for we had reached that level in our womanhood where we knew in our hearts that she would marry Yeshua and I was to be the confidant and friend to both of them.

I believe that every woman needs a female best friend. Mary Magdalene and I were in that category—best friends. We told each other everything. We told of our dreams, aspirations, hopes, and fantasies. We rejoiced in each other's happiness. The years passed while Yeshua was still off on his travels, and I more and more created a different life for myself. Since any communication had to come by word of mouth in that ancient era, words from him or about him were few and far between.

Therefore, dear Readers, this first chapter closes the first chapter on my life—the chapter where I was the little girl who grew into a woman, for at the age of sixteen we were considered women.

*Good morning, my beloved, we come to you during the beautiful music. **I AM Yeshua**. You have taken out your new binder for this book and I have been reading with you the different transmissions we have given. Let us now continue the book and again Mariam will come in. The first chapter was when we had collected bugs. I had forgotten that, and yes, it was an amusing time—an innocent time in our childhood. Now let Mariam come forward for the next chapter.*

THE HEALING

Good morning, my dear one, I am back to give you our second chapter for the book.

I, **Mariam**, am now what was considered in those days a grown woman of sixteen or so years. There was a handsome man whose attention I was beginning to feel and reciprocated. His name was Nathaniel. He was a kind man and generous, older than I, and we fell in love. While I still loved Yeshua, I knew I was not meant to marry him. Being practical and actually with a great deal of common sense, I turned toward another man. Our love grew stronger, and we loved and deeply cared for each other.

We were married in the Hebrew tradition. Therefore, when Yeshua finally came back, I was a married woman. He was somewhat surprised since it is human nature not to realize that time marches on. He was doing all the things he needed to do and perhaps did not think that time marched on for me too. He was quite delighted to know that Nathaniel and I had found each other, for he had always enjoyed Nathaniel's friendship.

Babies came in the early years of marriage for most people in that era. Of course, there were people who did not become pregnant for several years. In my case I became pregnant shortly after our marriage. I was delivered of a beautiful baby boy, who we named Benjamin. He had the large brown eyes—my eyes, actually—but he had his father's stature, tall and supple. As with most parents after their baby is born, we looked him over and checked him out to be sure everything was perfect—in perfect working order.

It was to our great sorrow to see that one of his little wee feet was deformed. It turned inward and did not lay flat. It was what doctors would call a *clubfoot*, so that when he walked, he walked on the side of his foot, which made him limp quite badly. If that was not enough, he also had an energetic nervous disorder so that he jerked and wobbled a bit. However, Nathaniel and I would hold our new son, love him, and croon to him. In addition, we prayed. We prayed that God would heal him. The years passed and he was not healed. He was not healed for several years.

I suppose one could say that it was our karma. The three of us were bringing forth karma from past lives and Benjamin had agreed to have a disabled body. We had agreed to have a disabled son. It was a time for us to strengthen our *faith and trust*—never to lose sight of the fact that if it were God's Will He would heal him in some way. It was so difficult.

You see, Readers, it seems as if I brought forward so much to deal with, to transmute into the Light—the grief that I suffered. As I look back, I would see the grief from my mother's death. When Yeshua left for those many years, there was the grief of our separation. Then some joy would come into my life, like my wedding, and the joy would come into my life with my beautiful little son. Then the grief would come again and waves of sorrow would wash over us (*tears*), for now we had this beautiful little boy who was quite severely disabled. However, he was a joy to our lives. He was so aware. At times, I think he was more in touch with God than we were. He also liked bugs (*chuckle*). Often he would bring in a little bug and exclaim, *Mommy, Mommy look!* He would feed it leaves and watch it eat. He had an expansive heart and everybody loved him. So many times when disabled people go out among humanity, the person is shunned in some way. People are uncomfortable to be around a disabled person. However, with Benjamin, people gravitated to him, for he had an extraordinary Light that blazed forth.

One day Yeshua came to visit. We were all so delighted. He came in the late afternoon, so we invited him to stay for supper and to spend the night. He gladly accepted and teased me as to whether I had turned out to be a good cook or not, or were there any bugs in the food (*smile*). I assured him I was a fine cook and no, I did not cook up any bugs. We joked with each other, sat down and had a delightful evening.

28

The Ultimate Experience
THE HEALING

When the hour came when we all needed to go to bed—especially Benjamin—and since it was such a warm night, Yeshua offered to carry up the sleeping pallets and put them on top of the roof for him and Benjamin. They kissed us goodnight and then went up to the rooftop. They did much of what Yeshua and I would do as children. They put their pallets down in a V shape where their heads were near each other. They looked at the stars and talked. As Yeshua often did, he laid on his back, crossed his leg, and pumped it up and down as he spoke. His words became softer and slower paced until he could perceive that Benjamin had gone to sleep. Yeshua stayed awake quite a while, mentally talking to God, and mentally talking to the Higher Part of Benjamin. Then he too fell asleep.

The sun rose early and they were awake by the time the cock crowed, to put it in those words—they were awake. Benjamin energetically popped up, as he was prone to do and excitedly talked to Yeshua who was awake now also. He sat up and looked at Benjamin, kind of smiling, waiting for Benjamin to come to the realization that he had been healed. His foot was no longer turned in. It laid flat. His jerks and great shivers had stopped. Yet, Benjamin was so used to ignoring his disabilities that he did not realize at first that he no longer had them.

When Benjamin did realize he had been healed, he went rapidly down the stairs yelling, *Momma, Father, look I am healed. God healed me!* He did not know that it was Yeshua's energy field and the love that Yeshua carried that had healed him also. Yeshua said nothing, but grinned, just grinned and his eyes sparkled. However, I knew and I rushed into his arms and whispered *thank you, thank you, thank you, dearest brother.* Then I would rush back, hug Nathaniel, and then hug Benjamin. I just kept hugging and hugging and hugging. Nathaniel was speechless, for he had no idea that that was the real reason for Yeshua's visit. He came to heal my son (*spoken tearfully*). He came to heal my son.

Therefore, Readers, what can I add to that? When you read in your Bibles about the miracles that Yeshua performed throughout the years, I do not believe that it is written that he had healed my son. After Yeshua left, Nathaniel, Benjamin and I clasped hands and gave thanks to God, for it was with His help and the Holy Spirit combined with Yeshua's love that had accomplished this miracle. Benjamin went on and had a happy life. He married and had children of his own.

You see, Readers, some people bring heavy karma at the beginning of their life, while others will end their lifetimes with heavy karma. Benjamin had accepted his, kept his joy and love of everyone until his own miracle happened. Know that the miracles that you read about in the Bible are Truth. The healings are Truth. People are apt not to believe in the healing miracles today, simply because you do not hear about them that much, other than your more famous Evangelists' Crusades and their healing miracles. As for the majority of people, they do not realize that healing miracles are Truth—that they still happen.

Benjamin speaks: Hello Readers, I am Benjamin, the son of Mariam and Nathaniel. During the first ten years or so of my life, I was known as the crippled son of Mariam and Nathaniel. However, since I was born that way I did not know any difference. I could see other children playing, but it is not as if this condition came after I had been normal. When you are born with it, in reality, you do not know the difference. You see you walk differently and jerk, whatever, but you have always been that way. Therefore, when you advance in years, you accept it. Since I was so loved, it was almost as though it did not matter to my parents either. They let me do what I could do. If I spilled something as I attempted to carry it, they allowed that to happen and would just wipe up after me.

My father would swoop me up and carry me on his shoulders. He would run with me so I would have the experience of running. It was like being on horseback or a donkey's back and running. My life actually was quite full. I played with the other children and had my lessons. I was intelligent—at least that is what my parents said. I had what I thought was a normal childhood life, for love made all the difference, as you know. I was especially fond of my Uncle Yeshua, for he was kind and I never felt like a cripple around him. He would tell me stories, his parables, as he was known to do. I then would have to tell him the meaning of what he was teaching me. In that way I was taught also. We had a very loving relationship.

It was with excitement that I went up to the rooftop with him to sleep, for I knew I would have him all to myself. I could pester him with questions. He had infinite patience and would answer my entire little boy queries. I think he told me stories just to keep me quiet, for I had a mind that was insatiable. I wanted to know about everything. The night that he healed me, I had a dream.

I saw myself walking in a beautiful meadow. I seemed to be walking without a limp and without a jerk. I remember in the dream it was such a beautiful sunny day. I seemed to have had a purpose in my going rapidly toward something—as if there were something I would need to do. I remember feeling joyous. The light was bright and golden as the sun can be. I did not marvel that I was walking in such a healthy way, for in the dream I did not remember that I had trouble walking. Now I know that my dream was showing me that I would be healed. At the time in the dream, I did not know it.

The rest happened pretty much as my mother has told you, the feeling of awe that I had been healed. Keep in mind, Readers, that those healing miracles were actually more accepted than they are today—especially after Yeshua became better known as he wandered the countryside. The people would just follow him. They were magnetized to him. Now whether the story (*in the Bible*) about the woman who touched his gown and got healed is true or not, I do not know. I only know that many people were healed as he paused a moment to talk to them and they reached toward him and touched a part of him. It is very possible that the story in the Bible is correct. There are many stories that were not scribed, including mine. We as a family were very open in telling that I had been healed. However, we attributed it more to God, than we did to Yeshua at that time. Remember, when you are living history, you are not that conscious as to what is going on in that history. We would hear stories and see them, but we were not aware of everything.

As the years passed, my memory of that time stayed sharp and clear. I thanked God in my daily prayers and gave Yeshua brotherly-type hugs. That is all I wanted to say today—that it was real. It was very real.

All right, dear one, we will close this chapter. Adieu.

The Ultimate Experience

OLD MYTHS REVISITED

Yeshua speaks: I must tell you, Readers, that some of the information you have read in your Bibles or elsewhere and have heard all of your lives simply are not true. In this book, we are helping you to come closer to Truth, as in that saying, *the truth shall set you free.* Now in those Biblical times there were dark days, as you know, where the government and the priesthood were feeling threatened by me, especially as the people kept proclaiming me as the new king. They did not realize that when I was speaking about the Kingdom, I was speaking of God, the God in their hearts.

I was no threat to them, but they did not know that. As with everything else, as the Light is coming to transmute the dark, the darkness always acts up. It does not want to let go of the control. It was pretty much the same way in those days; they did not want to let go of their control. They felt very threatened by the new Rabbi in their midst.

What I would like to address today is the whole Judas story, for as it is written, it is not Truth. Judas was a friend of mine—actually a childhood friend. He had a quick mind, as did I. Therefore, we had great fun talking and playing with each other as we came up with different ways to tackle a problem. We grew up together into adulthood. Since Judas was well educated, as was I through my many travels to parts of Europe and into India and Egypt, we were more sophisticated than, say, a *fisherman.* Now that does not make us better. It just meant we had a wider view of the world. Since Judas was educated and had a good aptitude for mathematics, I assigned him the role of being *treasurer* of our group. I was gathering the Disciples together, who later became the Apostles. He did an excellent job of controlling the money that came our way. The people would pay a little for this and that. We never asked for anything. They would just give it to us. We had

33

our needs taken care of by God. However, there was some money for miscellaneous items. Judas was in charge of all of that.

As there became an underground swell with the threat that I was going to usurp different peoples' positions, I was hauled into court, you could say—actually, in front of the Rabbis. They were upset with some of my teachings, for they did not understand them. On the other hand, I was tolerant of their position, for I could understand where they were coming from. However, when someone is threatened, many times it brings out the worst in people. I was taken to the authorities, and it dragged on to where it became quite nasty. The Bible says that Judas, you could say, *sold my identity* for thirty pieces of silver. That is total fabrication. **It never happened**. I know this is shocking to people, but it never happened.

I did not have to be pointed out. People knew me. One day when I was taken before a group of Rabbis, and then taken before the Roman government, I was severely reprimanded and told *get out and leave this area, for if you don't you will be crucified. Get out and take your wife with you!* I knew that they meant it. I knew that they would try to kill me in whatever way they could, if not by crucifixion, by any other means. They used poisons a great deal in those days. I could be poisoned or stabbed in the back. Death happened all the time. They had no forensic laboratories in those days, of course. Many times the body just was dumped somewhere and no one knew what had happened. It could be no different for me. It could very well happen to me.

I prayed long and hard. I prayed! I struggled, *what is it that you want me to do, Father? What is my purpose? What do you want me to do?* You see, Readers, this is where it will become difficult for you because the church fathers have brainwashed everyone. They actually have told the stories in the way that they wanted the outcome to be. It simply is not true. Your modern day Evangelists have made much about my crucifixion. They have teachings on the Crucifixion, what the stripes mean—*by His stripes, you will be healed*—what the blood means. They would

34

not be able to accept any of this. This is only something they may find out after they have died. Therefore, they will not agree that everything I am saying is Truth. They will say that the author is channeling a dark entity or is in fantasy. I assure you, Readers, she checks me out all the time, as we have taught her to do. She checks me out.

Therefore, what I am going to say to you may rattle you to the depths of your soul. I hesitate to tell you, for it grieves me. It grieves me, because you have been living this lie for so long. It is just deeply grieving for me. I have wanted for so long to set the record straight. Respected writers of books, even the previous books we gave this author...we carried on a tradition, you see, we carried on the fable that Judas betrayed Jesus. It did not happen, Readers. It simply did not happen. The Bible and the movies tell about the beating and flailing that I received. It is not Truth. The stories tell about my carrying that dreadful cross. It is not true. The stories tell about other criminals that were crucified, and yes, they were, but I was not among them. It was not true. The stories tell about the Marys gathered at the foot of the cross. It is not true. My dearest Readers, the anguish that I have in telling you this has this channel in tears, as she feels my grief. I only can say it bluntly. I did not carry the cross for my crucifixion, for **I was not crucified.** I was not crucified, dear Readers. **I was not nailed to any cross**. I was not! In fact, I listened to God and left the country, just as I had left for Egypt years before when Herod was killing all the babies. I again left. One could say that I ran for my life, for God told me to leave.

Joseph of Arimethea was a part of this. He helped. It was simplified in some ways, for I left with my wife, Mary Magdalene, who was pregnant with our baby girl. We went to Egypt where little Sarah was born. Readers, I can well imagine what you must be going through. When this author first heard of this... actually, she had read it a year or so ago but cannot remember where. She did not believe it, so she did not retain it. However, she had been drawn to read the Matthew Books. In the book, *Illuminations*

The Ultimate Experience
OLD MYTHS REVISITED

for a New Era, by Suzanne Ward (2003, pgs. 194-200), God tells Suzanne Ward that I had not been crucified. I give Suzanne Ward credit for her courage to write those words from God.

I can well imagine what you are going through, dear souls. I do not think there is anything that I can liken it to in order to give you an example of when a myth is brought to light. The myth about Santa Claus, perhaps, is as close as I can come to it, but that is too frivolous and not at the depth that I am sure this is since it touches everyone. You see, Readers, it is time. It is time that this information comes out. We could almost end the book here, for I know that many of you will not continue reading it. However, I say to you, know that we are talking about belief systems. Know that it is time to let those belief systems go, for they are holding you back. I believe it was God in the Introduction chapter who told you that your belief systems would hold you back. One of the biggest trials is the belief system that people have with religions. I would say that is the number one hurdle. I am afraid it will take several generations for these myths to be transmuted.

They are just too big—too big a lie. Therefore, you see the breadth of this includes all of the Disciples, those who wrote for the Bible, all the churches that are involved—probably the Catholic Church, which is one of the largest. We can only say that we grieve for you. Your anguish is our anguish. The crosses that people have in their homes, the crosses that people wear around their necks, all are associated with the crucifixion that never happened.

Now some of the crosses, like the Aquarian cross, have equal arms and are a spiritual symbol that is actually in the Heavenlies. It is Heaven and Earth joining, not the death of a person. There are so many religious icons, stained glass windows, statues, monasteries, and nunneries. It is a way of life. Probably those who are Buddhists will have an easier time of it, for that spiritual practice is not founded on the cross. People will say, *well what about the resurrection and Easter; what about the Ascension; what about books that write that you did not die on the cross, but went to Joseph of Arimethea's tomb and the women cleaned your body; you had the Shroud of Turin...what about all of that?* That is what I mean about the sorting out of the belief systems. It is not true.

That is all I wish to say, dear ones. That is all I wish to say. **I AM Yeshua.**

The Ultimate Experience

SETTING THE RECORD STRAIGHT

Good morning, my dear one, **I AM Yeshua.** We thought that since yesterday's transmission was on quite a heavy subject for you that it probably needed clarification for you also. Therefore, I have come back with, one could almost say, a part B to this. There are questions that swirl around in your mind. I will choose them one at a time. One of the questions is *did I have time to teach the Disciples before I left? Were all of them in on this?* In other words, Matthew, Mark, Luke, and John wrote their books after I left. Yes, I did have the opportunity to teach the Disciples. This is what I was doing. It was not until...one could almost say that the story goes that I went to the cross at the age of thirty-three. Therefore, yes, I left the country during that period.

The point I am making is that everything was already in place. The Disciples had been trained. They knew how to carry on. They were shocked, for it would be similar in this day and age to have a teacher and a leader who was respected and all of a sudden, the teacher says, *OK, I am now going off to Egypt. You are on your own.* Consequently, it was a difficult time for everyone.

Another one of your questions is *what about the Last Supper? Da Vinci painted the Last Supper.* There **was** a type of "last supper." However, it was not because I was going to be destroyed, or Judas was going to point me out. It was our last gathering together before we left on our trip. Therefore, there was a last supper; there were quite a few people present, and we had it in that upper room. However, you see it is so ingrained in people that I went to the cross and died on the cross, none of which I did, that many artists afterwards painted their renditions of my purported experience. Da Vinci was no different. He did paint in all of the codes that are supposed to be in his painting, and that is Mary Magdalene on my right. He did know who were sitting at that table. We crammed in as many as we could and there were still people all over the room. I think it is purported to be one hundred and fifty people or something, but the room could not hold that many. However, there were a great many.

Now, you thought, *what about the Eucharist, the Holy Communion? Did I drink the wine and say this is my blood? Did I break the bread and say this is my body?* Ah, we have another myth, don't we? That all stemmed from the Catholic Church for that was **their** ritual, their tradition that the church fathers had made up. *Drink my blood and eat my bones. (Sigh)* I am sorry, dear Readers. This is not true. I did not say that and that was not the ritual at our table. There was no chalice. We merely had our regular cup-ware, no glass. They were made out of pottery and probably had some chips on them here and there. That cup was not saved. Again, that is all made-up. In fact, Readers, if you took everything about all of that—being betrayed at Gethsemane and the Last Supper in the upper room, the Eucharist—I am afraid that was all made up. That was made up by the church fathers. The Disciples played into this also, for none of this was written until years after I had gone. None of that is true.

Consequently, I have laid another bombshell, shall we say. In the last chapter, you learned that I did not go to the cross. I left the country. Now you are learning there was none of the symbolic blood drinking or the body eating. It simply is not true.

Another question that is swirling around in your mind, dear channel and probably in the Readers', is that there has been written many times about a person named Sarah who came from Egypt. She had very dark skin. People could not quite place who she is. She has been a mystery. Well, that was Sarah, our daughter. She lived in Egypt. She played outdoors, so the sun beat down on her and she was very tan. Again, the church made her into a deity and called her the Black Madonna, whereas she was just our tanned, precious daughter.

Now Readers, you have a choice to make—or choices. Look at your belief systems and see if there are not some that you can let go of. There is an easy way to sort them out. If these are belief systems that you were taught in Sunday school, or if you had religious parents, then those beliefs are suspect. It is time to let them go. You see, in this day and age there is little that is the pure Spirituality. It is all religious dogma. Christianity needs to be rewritten because there is so much incorrect dogma.

There also is too much emphasis on asking the Saints to intercede for you in prayers. Why do you not just ask God? He is in your heart. He knows everything. Why do you need to ask a Saint? You see again, that is all Catholicism. It might surprise you to know that many of you were Saints in your past lives. It seems to be one of the paths souls take. *I think that in my next lifetime I will be a Saint. I will have to be martyred.* Back in antiquity you were burned or beheaded or something like that, with your refusing to disavow God, and then you were made a Saint. Then there were miracles that were said to be in your name. So and so prayed to you, Saint So and So, and you heard the prayer and answered it and the person received a miracle. That is rather suspect right there—not the miracle, but who answered the prayer—how about God or your Highest Self? I would imagine that those two answered your prayer.

Many people pray to me whom they call *Jesus.* I hear many of the prayers, and then I work with your Higher Self and ask God, *Is it in this person's timing that this prayer be answered?* You realize that this does not take weeks, months, and years. We do all this type of communication almost instantly. Nevertheless, I check in with your Higher Self and God before I help you. I will walk with you and I will support you. I will whisper words of encouragement into your mind. You may not realize it. However, I do not heal you, per se. You heal yourself or bring to yourself whatever you are asking. I just help with the communication. I take the request to your Higher Self, the diamond part of you, the monad part of you, your I AM Presence. I am very busy going between you and your Higher Part.

I believe I have covered most of what is swirling in this channel's mind. I said yesterday I was not beaten or flailed. Well,

I was kicked around a bit. It got quite nasty. They did punch me a bit, whip me a bit, and yes, it hurt, and yes, I bled. And yes, they convinced me they meant what they had said, for there was no love in their hearts, and they were mean men. To them people were disposable. If you raised too much of a ruckus and got too well known, they got rid of you. This book is not political, so I will not go into what your modern-day government is doing, but there are dark forces there! Many a person has been killed to get him or her out of the way. I know this is as hard for you to accept as the lies are about me. However, it is true. **I AM Yeshua**.

Mariam: Hello my dear ones, **I AM Mariam**. It is with great sorrow, dear Readers that the time has come for me to address some issues of which Yeshua has just been speaking. When we started this book, we did put our heads together. We knew this was the time that we would speak about the different myths—put a crack in them and break them up. Many people will not be able to face them. However, by reading this book, there **is** now a crack in your beliefs, so that your mind will return to them every once in a while, with the possibility of *oh gosh, maybe it's true*. Some belief systems are entrenched in stone, especially when it has to do with religion.

There was a large void in our lives when Yeshua and his wife, Mary Magdalene, left. At first there is that feeling—it is not excitement, but unrest and a concern. All we wanted was to get them out of the country, to get them to where it was safe. Again, there was the loss and there was the grief. I was losing my best friends, Mary and Yeshua. I clung to them. I must admit I was sobbing. My sorrows just all came up again, one loss after the other. A part of me was glad they were getting away safely. At least I hoped it would be safe. I just did not know when I would see them again. I did not know. Again, it was another stealthy trip, leaving at dusk. Mary was not that far along in her pregnancy, so she was able to walk and ride a donkey. It still was a long, difficult trip, but oh the void that was left behind.

The Ultimate Experience
SETTING THE RECORD STRAIGHT

Humanness has that feature when you know that people are near who you can go to for comfort, or just to be in their presence—to see them. You feel that loss when they go, even if you did not see them that much when they were near you. Then when they leave, you think *oh, when will I see them again?* We are speaking of the human body. I felt as if one of the pillars of my strength had left. Of course, I know that is not true. I carry my own strength, but that is how I felt. *What will I do without them—my confidants—Mary, my cherished friend and confidant, for woman talk and conversations, and Yeshua, my brother, for spiritual depth. What will I do without them? I loved them so and missed them so.*

A problem arose of course, because since there were no radios or television, the people did not know what had happened to Yeshua. They would say *where is Yeshua? I have not seen him.* We were very open in telling people they had gone to Egypt. In fact, we told them that he was told to leave the country by the government. Why keep that a secret? The government needs to know that he has left. It was not an easy transition for the Disciples, however.

There is another story that circulates with Saint Paul, and all the letters he wrote. I will not get into that, but be suspicious, Readers. Be suspicious. Did he write all of them?

The aftermath was quite despondent for us. I am including my Mother Mary in that. You can only imagine what she was feeling—relief that he had escaped, but sorrow for she did not know when she would see him again.

Therefore, Readers with that we will close this chapter. I wonder how many of you are still reading and wondering what we are going to come up with next. Well, since the book has barely been started, I would say, *keep reading and tune in.*

This is all for now

I AM Mariam. Adieu.

THE QUESTIONS CONTINUE

Yeshua: This chapter will be about the sorrow that takes place—the sorrow of parting, for you see we also were in grief when we had to leave many relatives and friends behind. The questions continued. We did not know if we would meet again, for we would have to go to them, or they would have to come to us. We did not have that information at that time. Therefore, we too experienced sorrow. In some ways, we experienced relief—to be out from under that regime where there is no tolerance for new ideas.

It was not only the Roman government, you see, but my own people, the Hebrew priests and the Rabbis. They carried no tolerance. They were so rigid in their thinking, so rigid in that this was the only way one could live—no work on the Sabbath. Those ancient edicts had no flexibility. Therefore, for someone like me who proclaimed to be a Rabbi, which I was, and then not to follow these laws to the letter was considered blasphemous, a direct defiance to the Sanhedrin. They did not realize that they did not leave room to contemplate that *well these laws need to be looked at again. Maybe they need a new interpretation.* There was no flexibility and no room for a new point of view. It always amazed me, and I do not know why. I ought to have been used to it by then. It amazed me that here were these grown men with so little flexibility that their own Laws were strangling them and they could not see it! People were ostracized. They still could not see it.

The story of my Mary, Mary Magdalene, being stoned, having been caught in a compromising position with another man, simply is not true. However, the way it is written in the Bible, again by the male scribe—was that it was always the males who condemned the person, yet they themselves had gone to prostitutes! There was just no logic to it. My Mary was never a prostitute. She was never a fallen women and never had seven demons taken out of

43

her. I did not do that. It is beyond me as to where they came up with those stories! I did not exorcise demons out of my Beloved. It is ridiculous! My Beloved had no demons (*sigh*).

However, some people were mentally ill, as with any civilization. You have your mentally ill and insane people. Some of those people were possessed. I am not saying that it did not exist; **it did not exist in my wife**. I do know that good people sometimes get in trouble when they play with fire—go to a dark entity for the experience and then get caught. There is so much in the Bible, dear Readers. You need to take all those books in the Bible—Matthew, Mark, Luke and John—read them, take the wisdom from them, and let go of the parts that seem a little unbelievable to you, for they probably are.

Therefore, Christianity did have a wobbly birthing. I had taught the Apostles, but many times they did not understand what I was talking about either (*smile*). Further on in later years, they tried to explain it as best as they could, but their interpretations simply are not true. *I say woe is me when the churches get hold of all of this.* They would in their minds say *well I guess he must have said this*—the assumptions, the assumptions. There was no end to these. They are so amazing.

In this modern time, the Christian faction is dominant in the area known as the *Bible belt.* The Christian churches are very strong there. The Christian zealots have not kept their own house in order. We wrote about this in the other books. The morality of many of the people is lacking. They are stealing. There are power struggles. They carry a false joviality. *Everything is fine*, while they could be perpetrators abusing children. The church has become so dark. Dear Readers, the Christian church, as you know, is made up of many sects: Presbyterians, Methodists, Mormons, Pentecostals, and Baptists. Each one, and there are more—the *free lancers*—will call themselves the Christ Church of this or the Unity Church of that. The different names have changed throughout history. I will say not one of those sects is free of scandal.

44

If the Holy Spirit came along and blew behind the curtain of each person, people would be shocked. In other words, if people stood in front of a curtain that hid their morality, how they faced life, managed their home, and raised their children, and the Holy Spirit lifted that curtain, what would you see? What does God see? Does He see greed, selfishness, tyranny, control, miserliness, and stinginess? Just know if a person has a stingy nature, it is not just in money, but also in all of his emotions. These people have a very difficult time in giving out love. If the Holy Spirit moved behind your curtain, what would be found? On the other hand, maybe your curtain is transparent. Anyone can see through it, see who you are, how you act, how you behave, what you are like in your private moments, and see the purity, strength, the giving—all the attributes that make up the Christ Consciousness, that makes one shining brightly in the Light as a Wayshower for all to follow.

Here I AM Yeshua-Sananda, for I have blended with that Higher Part of me. We are surveying man-womankind. We had a conversation with God, questioning if this were the correct time to bring to the Light the lies that have been perpetuated on down throughout the ages. There were lies about me, my Mary, Mother Mary, Father Joseph, lies that did a great deal of harm. In the churches, the zealous conditions, the zealous state in order to control people, perpetuated the lies. It got so that they embellished each other. One told a lie and the other one told that same lie and added another one. It was a snowball effect. It then came down through generations, so that today people have to deal with the shock of finding out the truth at long last. People have been programmed so heavily throughout their childhood and in Sunday school, from parents and teachers. If you read the Bible, there are stories in the Bible that are not true. They are so programmed that there will be people who literally will not be able to see another point of view, will not be able to let go of that belief system.

We are speaking about traditions and holidays. The whole greeting card industry—all of those religious cards will have to be rewritten. It just fans out and out and out! There will be the questioning, the inner questioning, for it sets up such confusion in the minds of people. Even this channel questions, for she realizes that not everyone has the same timing for these revelations. Whom does she tell about this? She has told one daughter. Does she dare tell the other two, for they have different belief systems? You see it even gets into the family dynamics now. Families will have to teach their children differently, if they choose to believe what I am telling them. Of course, there will be people who will not have heard about this book and will not read it anyway. Think of all the questioning.

Therefore, you see, Readers, why it is not a simple thing to break up a lie-system that is as embedded as this one is. There is that saying *I am not going to do this; I will be crucified.* Well, can you not imagine what a book like this coming out when Dan Brown was put on the hot seat for *The Da Vinci Code*, saying that Mary Magdalene and I were married, which we were? *Dan Brown—right on!* Can you not imagine what it would be like for this author to put a book out that says *OK, scratch everything you have ever heard about Christianity? Jesus did not go to the cross. He was not nailed to the cross. His mother and father had a natural relationship. It was not a virgin birth. She was a virgin, but she married Joseph and they had a normal, loving, sexual relationship and brought in many children, including me.*

Here is another myth: Did I walk on water? Do you remember that one? Did I quell the storm in the fishing boat and walk on water? Actually, I did quell the storm, for I was able to control the weather, but not by any supernatural means, but simply because I was in tune with Nature and I was able to speak to the storm through Love and that did calm the waters. Did I ever walk on water? Control the energies and yes, you too can walk on water. Let us see; what else is out there? Oh, did I multiply the fishes for the fishermen. Yes, I did do that. I simply talked to the fish.

Now, let's see, did I multiply the bread and fish for the people to eat? Yes, I was able to do that also.

It is called *manifestation,* people. You can do this too. You have to study, learn, and raise your consciousness. You can do this. This is where the scribes did get it right. I kept telling the people *you can do this too!* To this day, you can do this. Each one of you has a Higher Self that can do this. This author has a rather amazing story where she awoke in the middle of the night a few years ago. She felt a paper clip in her hair. She thought that was rather strange, took it out, and went back to sleep. She saved the paper clip and still has it. She told her daughter, and her daughter tried to make it more logical. *Well maybe the hairdresser put it in*, but that actually did not sound very logical either, so that was pooh-poohed *(laughingly)*. Why would she go to get a haircut and leave with a **paper clip** in her hair? We thought that was very amusing. Where did the paperclip come from? It was manifested by her Higher Self, and actually it was a clue that she would be using paperclips in the not-too-distant future. That was a clue for her that she would be writing a book and clipping many papers together—which did happen—this is now the fourth book.

Therefore, you see, you can all do this—manifest—and the author has. Now she has not taken it a step further and manifested anything like a gemstone or a gold piece. If she knew how to do it, she could do it. Consequently, my manifesting more fish and bread for the people who had come to hear me speak and were hungry is true. I gave it to them. Now was it exactly as reported in the Bible? No. Is anything? Rarely is it. However, they reported the gist of it in a true way.

Dear Readers, I do know the quandary I have put you all in. I commend you for continuing to read. We put this controversial material in the beginning of the book, so as you kept reading, at least we hoped you would, the ideas would be repeated throughout the book. By the end of the book, perhaps, you would be more accepting and that will cause a crack in your belief systems so that you can start letting some of this go. Therefore, the ensuing chapters probably will mention it repeatedly. However, for now this is all I will say for this chapter.

I AM Yeshua.

The Ultimate Experience

MOTHER MARY SPEAKS

Yeshua here. We have another interest now—a new chapter. What we are going to do with this chapter is to bring forth Mother Mary who started all of this, the birthing of me! Therefore, we thought it only appropriate to have a chapter devoted entirely to her perception of this second flight into Egypt and all it entailed. I will now step aside and my Mother Mary will be speaking.

Good morning, my dear author, **I AM Mary**, or to you and the Readers, I would be **Mother Mary**, the Mother of my beautiful son, Yeshua. As you have surmised, he was quite an astounding son, a very curious little boy—all boy. However, all of my children were curious and I loved them all dearly, as I loved Mariam, the wounded Mariam who we took into our family and into our hearts.

We had known Mariam quite well, actually, while we were all at Mount Carmel. Therefore, it was not as if we were adopting a stranger. We were adopting family. That term *adoption, or adopting,* is probably not that accurate. There was some legality to it, but it was more of an agreement between her father and us. *Yes, she may stay with us.* We were her family.

We knew that Mariam had a role to play in our family; both Joseph and I felt this and knew this. In those days, we did not think in terms of energy fields and Higher Souls and so forth, but that was what was going on. Our lives needed her energy blending with ours. We had a purpose, and a great deal of that purpose was in helping the extraordinary son of ours, Yeshua. We saw that Mariam carried this *peace* in her that was most unusual. She was just peaceful to be around, but she could easily be wounded by unkind remarks that perhaps other children outside of my family would say to her—just as it is nowadays that children can be unkind and cruel.

The Ultimate Experience
MOTHER MARY SPEAKS

Mariam was quite sensitive. She did not always tell you what was going on in her mind or her emotional body. She would suffer inwardly, quietly, and keep it to herself. However, as she became more comfortable living in our family, she became more open. If I asked her, she then would tell me honestly what she was feeling. Therefore, I watched for that and knew when I needed to ask her what she was feeling; I would know she was struggling with something that needed to be told.

Her way of perceiving the world did not change that much after she got married. When Benjamin was born, he was a precious baby, as all babies are. He had that wee little deformed foot that would touch your heart. I would feel deeply for Mariam and Nathaniel. Therefore, when we would be together, I would question her. *Tell me what you are feeling, Mariam. How are you?* Then the dam would break and the emotions would flood out.

It was with such great joy when she told me that Yeshua and the Higher Part of Benjamin and God had healed him. I believe that with all the miracles my son performed, that that one has to be the one that touched me the most, for Benjamin was a fine, handsome lad. He had the looks of his father and mother and also her gentleness. To be able to see him run and play as a normal young boy was such a joy. We gave much praise to God and many a thank you to Yeshua who refused to take any credit for it, which was his way. He just kept saying *it was God's will and Benjamin's Spirit that created the healing.* Consequently, you can well imagine the agony and the pain that came upon all of us—the fright—when we saw how the Sanhedrin Rabbis were out to get Yeshua. They felt so threatened by him. We felt that they actually targeted him, tried to trip him up, and tried to get him to confess that he was being blasphemous. If only they knew that he was closer to God than they were. If only they knew that. However, it was not meant to be.

Actually, everything was in God's plan. All of this was set up before we were born. We knew that since we would be in human bodies that something had to happen that would propel Yeshua and his wife, Mary, to leave the area. As he brought in the new ideas, the Sanhedrin actually played right into his hands. They played their role that was assigned to them before they were born, to cast out this magnificent son of God that we all are, the sons and daughters of God, to cast him out of their midst and propel him to go on his way.

It was in Egypt where he was meant to be, for there were great Teachings there on the different planes and dimensions. Yeshua and Mary had great awakenings, or what you might call *Initiations.* Everyone played the roles that had been assigned to him or her. When you are in those higher dimensions, or we say the *Heavenlies,* and are working out your adventures for the next life, your game plans, it is somewhat easy for souls to forget that once they are in the body, they have their emotional body to deal with. You can come in fully aware, although most people are not, but you can come in aware, know your purpose, and then have to deal with the emotional body.

A great example would be your Mozart, that genius who played any instrument and composed practically from the time he was a toddler. He could do all of that. He brought that genius in with him. He was a Master. However, he had to deal with his emotions and was quite immature in his emotional field—quite immature. Therefore, in his next lifetime, he was dealing with his emotions. He did not bring his aptitude for music in quite that strongly, for he had to strengthen and calm the emotional body. When we are in the Heavenlies, we can forget what it is like to be in the body and have emotions we have to control.

Consequently, when Yeshua and Mary left, those of us who were left behind were hit with tremendous peaks and valleys of emotion—like we were on an emotional roller coaster. It was not until a few years later that we were able to journey to Egypt, have the grand reunion, and meet baby Sarah. Mariam, Nathaniel and I were able to go. There were others in our party, but we three had the true purpose for going. While there, we also studied and experienced the different dimensions. Many times we became a grounding aspect to help one of the others. It was a very enjoyable time in our lives. Joseph of Arimethea also would come occasionally, but he was a busy man, so he did not tarry too long.

I know that in this modern day, many stories swirl around about my last days and where I was, but for now, I think it suffice to say, I was able to visit my precious son, Mary, and baby Sarah, who was fast becoming brown as a little berry—just so cute, so cute. That is all I will say for now.

Thank you for honoring me in these pages,

I AM Mother Mary. Adieu.

The Ultimate Experience

DIMENSIONAL REALITIES

Good morning, our dear ones, we are a blend this morning of many of the characters that have been coming forth for this book. We will be talking about being in two realities and dimensions at the same time for this chapter. The fifth dimension will have a different reality than the third dimension. The third dimension will have a different reality than the fourth dimension. This channel is in the fifth dimension and touches into the sixth some of the time. Therefore, her reality differs from those who are winding up their lifetimes in the third dimension. That is why many times people cannot understand what she is saying and think of it as laughable. This is what will happen with this book, for this book is in a different reality, the higher dimensions, where none of the crucifixion, none of those stories is true.

As you know, humanity thinks of resurrection as being raised from the dead, whereas in reality, one is being resurrected all the time. It is just raising one's consciousness. However, if you were dead, it could also be raising you up from death. To people in the lower dimensions, however, resurrection is still religious and Biblical. We will say that resurrection is continuing. As for the Ascension, that happened when I, as Yeshua-Sananda, ascended while in old age. I was in the Kashmir area of India, when I drew to myself the ending of that lifetime. I then ascended. My Mary was not with me at that time, although there are some authors who write that she was. She was not. She was in France about which has been written. I will get into my death at another time, for it was not a true death in the physical sense. It was Ascension. I did not take my body with me at that time, for I had no more use for it. I just left it and rose. It was very rapid. I left my body in a simple grave, so that it would go back to the Earth in a true Jewish tradition. All of that will be addressed at another time.

For today's work, beloved, this book—this new reality—is progressing nicely. There will be people who will not agree with you—relatives, friends, and strangers. I am sure you are prepared for that. One of your questions is how do I control all of this? Do I just talk about it freely and let the chips fall where they may? On the other hand, do I need to be more careful? We would say follow your intuition. If you feel they can handle it, tell them. If it will be too severe a shock for them, do not tell them. They will know when your book comes out in the manuscript form, just like your previous ones. There will be people who will be shocked and it certainly will make them think. However, those people whose mentality and consciousness is still in the lower dimensions still will want to believe their truth.

Those authors, Claire Heartsong, Glenda Green, and Margaret Starbird, all wrote their books in the early 1990's. They received their information and wrote their books and then waited a while before publishing. Some published right away and some waited. Their information at that time was correct. The whole Anna, Grandmother of Jesus *book was Claire Heartsong's reality, not necessarily our reality, but hers. She did a beautiful job in writing it. We cannot negate her and say that none of that was true, for that was her reality at that time. It was her reality that she washed my body. It was her reality coming from the fourth dimension that I was crucified, but my dear soul, I was not! You were Mariam then and in that reality, you did help prepare the body. That was in that reality. However, the reality in which we are writing this book, Mariam never had to go through that. It simply did not happen.*

What we are talking about is physics, actually, the science of physics and the different realities that come from God. If you are in a particular dimension, you will have that reality and if you are in another dimension, you will have that reality. Everything is going on at the same time. That is what reality does. There is no structure; there is just focused energy making the reality. People will be struggling having read the other chapters; therefore, this one may explain it to them, whether they believe it or not is something else. They simply may not be able to get this lesson on

The Ultimate Experience
DIMENSIONAL REALITIES

Realities. When this author channels us, she is in the high fifth and touching the sixth dimension. Most channels need to get that high in order to channel us.

All right, beloved, I am going to bring in another Presenter for this chapter on Reality. He will introduce himself.

Good morning, my dear one, **I AM Joseph, the father of Yeshua.** Much was written about me that was not accurate either. The Bible refers to my teaching Yeshua, which I did, teaching him carpentry, and being the father of our brood, then dying more or less in the same area as I was. That is one reality. In the *Anna...* books, Claire writes that I was in the Himalayas. I had gone there for spiritual work. It was from there that I made my Ascension. That was another reality. Actually, that was the correct reality in my mind, as I did ascend from there. Which one is correct? It all depends on what dimension you are in. Those in the third dimension will believe the Bible. Those in the fourth dimension will believe that possibly I could have been in the Himalayas. Therefore, these different realities still exist today. Of course, the crucifixion was not played out repeatedly, but in that denser third dimension, people see that as happening. In the less dense reality, it never happened and our son left the country. We favor that reality.

When you are in a body, having worked out what you are going to be doing during that lifetime, unless you are very aware and have studied, you will not know about these different dimensions and realities—especially clear back then. However, our family was very aware. Yeshua knew; Mary knew. This author watched "The Passion of the Christ" by Mel Gibson last night. It was the first time she could bring herself to do so, for she had heard it was a very profound and somewhat gory movie and she just could not bring herself to watch it previously. However, since her reality now is that Yeshua did not go to the cross, was not crucified, she was able to watch it with less trauma to her. She still questions about the flailing he received in the movie. NO, that did not happen to that degree. He was whipped a few times, but no way near what the movie showed. The movie shows him as a bloody mess! But no, in our reality that did not happen. However, the movie did make her think and she kept repeating to herself *thank God, it did not happen. Thank God, it did not happen.* However, it did happen to criminals. It was a very cruel way to punish in those Roman times. I had already made my transition when all of this took place in that reality. This may surprise you but we watched the crucifixion from the higher dimensions, what you might call *Heaven or Nirvana.* This epic affected all of us, even while in Nirvana.

The question is coming up from the channel *what about Judas? I know that he did not betray the Lord, but did he commit suicide?* Ah, this is where it becomes complicated because, yes, he did take his own life. He was in anguish. Much of what was reported before the actual cross experience in that reality had already taken place. **Judas did not betray Yeshua**, but he did nothing to help either. When the Sanhedrim came and took him away for questioning, Judas felt guilty. In the reality where Yeshua and Mary had to flee the country again, remorse filled Judas.

You see, Readers, Judas would have taken his life no matter what went on. It was known in the Heavenlies that he would take his life. It is written that when he comes out of that deep grief, he by that act will affect the whole Universe, because that grief is in that third-dimension reality. This is going to be difficult for Readers to separate and to understand. Therefore, know that I did die as written in that third dimension in the area where we lived. However, I died in the Himalayas, as Anna had said and made my transition into a higher dimension.

That is all I wish to say, dear Readers. Thank you for the privilege of speaking with you.

I AM Joseph.

The Ultimate Experience

GRANDMOTHER ANNA

I AM Yeshua, dear one. I will introduce a different character for our book. The book is proceeding quite nicely and we are most pleased. Now the tone will change just a bit, for we wish to maintain a high level of frequency for the book and not let it dip too low with some of these astounding revelations. Let me step aside now and let the person step forward.

Hello our dear one, I AM Anna, your grandmother. (Oh, my heavens, Anna, are you sure you have the right channel (laughingly). Ought it not to be Claire?) We thought it would be appropriate for me to come, for you have read my book through Claire Heartsong and now you have me for these few pages. The reason for my coming is to help validate that, yes, you are bringing forth a book from the higher dimensions. For Readers who do not quite understand the higher and lower of dimensions, I can put it into the terms of reaching into the future. You have heard that past, present, and future are all happening simultaneously. When I wrote the book Anna, Grandmother of Jesus, *I wrote it from the fourth dimension. We will call it the lower end of the fourth dimension, for I needed to reach a certain population of Readers. It has been very well received, and I am quite gratified.*

When I met this channel at a seminar in Tucson a year ago, I told her that she had been at Mount Carmel. I did not tell her, however, that she also was my granddaughter, Mariam, for that would have been too shocking for her. I noticed that she did not ply me with questions. She was respectful of my presence and felt it was not appropriate to question me at that time. Therefore, Yeshua asked me to come forth to speak as his grandmother. You see it does not make any difference if I am speaking to you from the third or the fifth dimension, for I am still Yeshua's and Mariam's grandmother.

57

The Ultimate Experience
GRANDMOTHER ANNA

When you have your own father and mother in this modern time, it makes no difference to you whether one's soul is in one dimension or another. You live your life the way that you had agreed. At least we hope that you have and are doing that. Is it not an interesting theory that Mariam was with me during the reality of the crucifixion and now I am speaking through her, this channel who carries the aspect of Mariam in these modern times? Readers, you have no idea how intricate, how complex this Theory of Reality is. One needs to be as ancient as I am with many lifetimes before one has a true sense of the realities.

You see I know Mariam in both realities. I knew Mariam at Mount Carmel in the third dimension, but in the fifth dimension, the Essenes have actually moved on. Everything changes when there is a finer density—**everything** changes. Just as you have heard that there are new chakras and colors coming in, will that not change your perception? You do not even have a name for them yet. There are flowers on Nirvana that are the most magnificent colors, and you do not have the vocabulary for them yet. It is a different reality.

It may interest you to know that the emotional body will change also in a different reality, the finer reality. People who may have been cruel or unkind in the third dimension, and then as they evolve, those more negative emotions are transmuted into Love frequencies. Then when their consciousness reaches the fifth dimension, they are different. The people are different. The Evangelists many times say that Jesus is the same today as yesterday and he will be the same tomorrow. They say this repeatedly. It makes no sense to us, for Yeshua is not the same. No one is. At least we hope he is not the same—we know he is not, for we must always be evolving and growing in order to keep our energies flowing freely and loving and Light. You are not the same today as you were yesterday and will not be the same tomorrow, for you will grow; you will change. If you are growing in consciousness, then we could say that you are being resurrected. It is the consciousness that is growing, and therefore,

58

you are not the same, nor is Yeshua the same. In fact, he is more of his Light body now, the Lord Sananda Kumara, than he was when people knew him as Yeshua. One does not have to be quite so technical when speaking about Yeshua-Sananda. They are one.

Therefore, when I had written my experience from the third and lower fourth dimension, **that** was the Reality caused by humanity. It was never God's will, never God's will. The Hebrew was programmed to give sacrifices to God. They were always sacrificing the animals. There is the story about Abraham agreeing to sacrifice his son, Isaac. No, that is not correct. That story is fabrication. It always rather amazes me how distorted some of the pure Teachings have become. They were distorted by the church fathers. It was as if they were writing their own little fiction books. Some were a more graphic fiction than others were. God never would sacrifice his son.

One of His commandments was *thou shalt not kill,* so why would He give Abraham the instruction to **kill** his son Isaac even as a test, or have Yeshua sacrificed on the cross—to sacrifice his life for humanity? That is what humanity thought and created. However, you see that when you get into the higher dimensions, the high fifth dimension where this book is being created, these baser creations of sacrificing to save someone simply are not true. They are not true.

This author is frequently attempting to find the logic in something. When something is not logical for her, she is unable to accept it. She could believe and one time did that Yeshua was crucified, but not because he was dying for everyone else' sins, but he was crucified by an angry mob and jealous Rabbis. Again, this was third dimensional reality that I described in my book.

We do not see how humanity is going to be able to make this transition very swiftly. As you know, evolution is very slow. Therefore, there will be those who will refuse to believe anything of this nature—that **the crucifixion did not happen**. There is just too much riding on it. There is even an entire commercial industry riding on it—all the jewelry crosses. I believe that Yeshua has mentioned this.

That is about all I wish to say my dear one, but I wanted you to know that your grandmother was part of this book, also. *What did I call you?* You called me actually, *Grandmother Anna*, for I called your adopted Mother, *Mary Anna*. In order to separate the two Anna's you called me *Grandmother Anna*. I usually called you *Mariam*, although there were times I called you *Mari*, also. You can see there were different interpretations swirling around the names. You were greatly loved, Mariam. *Thank you, Grandmother Anna.* I will step back now. I will not come again, but just know that my energies are also a part of this book. *Thank you, Grandmother.* Adieu.

The Ultimate Experience

FATHER-MOTHER GOD SPEAKS

I AM Yeshua, my dearest one, and I wish you a Happy Fourth of July 2006. (Thank you, Lord, I wish it were a peaceful one.) *We do too. We do too. As you heard in the prayer yesterday of The Christ Matrix, America needs to pray for Israel. It is heating up again. This time the terrorists are truly inflaming the Palestinians. They come into that blessed country with evil in their hearts. As you know, that whole area, that whole Middle East area is the heart chakra of the planet. When the Christ asks for special prayers for Israel, then you know that something very dark is planned for that area. Therefore, something very dark is happening to the heart of the planet. That is all I will say, but pray not only for America, but also for Israel, that blessed land.* (And now in 2012, you still need to pray for her.)

If you are so inclined, you can have an Appendix and put Rowena's reading about the book into the Appendix. That way the Readers would have more of an insight of what went on in the creation of this book. We will keep the Appendix for writings that perhaps would not go into the body of the book. We will see.

You have a question about the dream you had this morning about the earthquake. I told you a year ago that a severe earthquake was coming for California. With the technology of the benevolent space ships, they were able to calm the Earth somewhat. However, now it is time. It must come. It still will not be what is feared as the "big one," but it will be severe. It looks to be on land, versus out to sea. It will kill people and it will frighten others to leave, which is rather amazing that people need to be frightened out of their shoes before they will pick them up and move on. We can never give you the exact date, for that is up to Mother Earth. However, it is building severely and we could say that it could happen anytime.

Now, were you surprised when Anna came in? (Yes, I was. It was very nice—two pages—very nice.) *We thought that would be* *a treat for you. (*It was thank you.*) She definitely will be part of the book, for she is part of that Holy Family of which we all are, including you! We were also delighted that she chose to come.*

This may surprise you, but we thought it was about time to bring in your Father and by this we mean, God, for He has something He would like to add to what He had said previously. Without further comments, I will step aside so that our blessed Father can speak.

Father-Mother God speaks. And how is My precious daughter this morning? (*I am doing very well, Father; thank you so much for coming.*) It is our pleasure because as you know the Mother aspect is within Me also. Since in the book you have been speaking about realities, I wanted to add My comments to this. Realities are an energy that comes from Me. You call it perhaps, going into the past, present or NOW, and future. These are energies of reality. You woke up this morning, a reality. It is a reality that you had something to eat—breakfast—you broke your fast. That is a past reality. The present reality is you are channeling this book and I AM speaking to you and to the Readers. That is the NOW. The NOW also is that I AM in your heart. I am in the heart of all My sons and daughters. However, another reality is that I know and I see what you cannot. You were asking about a coming earthquake for California. I know it, I see it, I hear it, but that is what you would call a future reality, but what I would call a different reality from the NOW. It is moving into a finer density, a finer dimension, a higher one. Whenever anyone moves into the future, he or she is in a higher dimension. Nothing stays the same; everything is moving. Therefore, the new reality, or one that is even an hour ahead of this one of the NOW, could be where there will be an earthquake. We could say those are the realities of living in California—that there will be earthquakes. If the quakes are severe enough and are out at sea, they will trigger tsunamis, these huge waves of ocean waters that rush over the land. That is another reality. The reality of people

62

living in Californian is different from the reality of people living in Arizona.

Therefore, when we are speaking of realities, we are speaking of one's perception—how you perceive something. When We are speaking of the crucifixion in this book, that is in the lower density of the third dimension; and **the perception of people—their reality, their thoughts, their choices—make the crucifixion real.** Did I, God the Father, order My son to be nailed to the cross? **I did not.** Evangelists and religious Readers hear this: **I did not order my son to be nailed to the cross.** Never would I do that! That was the church fathers controlling the people, for they put out there that Yeshua chose to go to the cross to save humanity from its sins and therefore, if *you pray to Jesus he will save you. By his blood, you are washed from your sins.* I must say those church fathers certainly had an imagination—dark imaginations. You realize when I say *dark* it merely means there is no Light. Please keep in mind that since all of you are My children, I love you all, black, or white, dark or Light. I love you all, for you are My creations, My children. The Creator and I have given you your free will.

Therefore, back in that third dimension, that reality, the church fathers were expressing their free will and making their choices. *We will change a little of this and change a little of that. People do not need to know that. They will not understand that. We will say that he sacrificed himself, the son of God; he sacrificed himself to save humanity.* Well, **nothing could be further from the Truth.** Readers, if you but will accept this. Let your religious dogma go. Accept the Truths. **Jesus does not save anyone.** I will call him *Jesus,* for that is how most of you think of him, although he prefers to be called by his Hebrew name, Yeshua, and Jeshua for more modern times.

This man, this creation of Mine was so filled with Love and Light. I hope you realize by now that Love and Light are the same. If your body is 25% Light, that is how much Love you carry in your body. If your body is 80% Light that is how much Love you carry in your body. This is an interesting thought, is it not? Do you realize, Readers that the majority of humanity is not at that 25% Light? You have heard when something is at critical mass, 51% that something will happen—anything will happen if it is at critical mass. Some say that the Light and the Love in people's hearts in humanity is at critical mass and therefore, different energies on Earth can come forth. We do not see that as true yet. I wish it were, but it is not yet.

One can also use a measuring device when one is on the evolutionary ladder. We are speaking of Initiations. Some people who you thought were your great leaders, John F. Kennedy for example and there are others, had not reached the higher Initiations yet. It was the Master Djwal Khul, the Tibetan, who wrote in the Alice Bailey books that one must have taken the fifth and sixth Initiation before one had a **choice** as to return to Earth or not. The percentage of humanity that still has that choice is very low. Some of your great leaders of the past had not even reached the third Initiation. Then where do you think that puts humanity? The majority of humanity still needs to come back to Earth—to reincarnate. Now when I say that a soul does not have the choice to come back, I could have stated that differently, because the choice is always with the soul—again, the free will. However, there are some that dilly-dally, dawdle in Nirvana before they leap again into that dense third dimension energy to transmute their karma.

Those Masters who come into an Earth existence at a higher Initiation level make a **choice** to help humanity and to help Me, for they have these tasks to perform, you see. There is so much *negativity* on the planet that when these Masters choose to incarnate again, they willingly take on a chunk of others' karma. Each person's perception of this karma varies. The karma could be on a personal, familial level, as in taking on the different genetic illnesses that run in that family; or to take on the National karma where it could be in the political scene; or it could be world karma. It may have to do with being of service to the poorer countries. When you see these well known people going to some of the third world countries such as doctors to perform operations under very primitive conditions, they have taken on world karma. Movie stars who adopt third world babies of different ethnic cultures have taken on world karma. However, many times those babies they are adopting facilitate the ending of cycles from those past lives in those ethnic cultures.

There are many different realities, such as the reality of sacrificing. Crucifixion has been made into a metaphor. I believe it was Mary Magdalene who spoke of using the crucifixion as a metaphor in one of our books—our first book. (I am calling this author's books, *Our*, for she is writing books that I have commissioned her to write before she was born. You have heard this before, so I consider them Our books.) Mary Magdalene wrote about how crucifixion has become a metaphor for an expression in the English language. *I can't do that. I'll get crucified. I'll get nailed to the cross.* That was humanity's choice 2000 years ago. That happened 2000+ years ago—an angry mob, disgruntled Rabbis wanted to humiliate and nail an innocent man to a cross. For those of you who believe all of that third-dimension reality, at least take home to your hearts that he did not die at that time, no matter what has been said or written. **He did not die on the cross.** Read Claire Heartsong's book, *Anna, Grandmother of Jesus.* She does a superb job of describing those horrific scenes.

Let us travel in time 2000+ years ago to the present. Are you ready to change your belief systems, Readers, or are you still operating in the third-dimension mentality? Lift your sights; promote yourself; raise yourself up; climb up Jacob's ladder—in any way I can get the idea across. Bring some doubt in, even. Let go of the religious training you received, for most is not true. If the Earth is moving into the fourth dimension, it is hoped you are moving with it. However, many of you are still ending your third dimension reality, your third dimension mentality.

This book is coming from the higher fifth dimension. It actually touches the sixth. We are talking about consciousness.

The Ultimate Experience
FATHER-MOTHER GOD SPEAKS

We are talking about Light. When people hold this manuscript in their hands, they will be holding fifth-dimension energy. When they read this manuscript, they will be reading fifth-dimension words. You see, this author was told that it was very important to get the fifth-dimension energy, reality on paper—in printed form; it **anchors** it. When you bring in an idea, you bring in energy; you print it; it is on paper; you then have anchored it. There are many similar anchors around the world. Each is receiving information in his or her own way that in the fifth dimension, the crucifixion did not happen. That is a hard concept for people to get into their mental and emotional bodies. Is it not amazing that people would rather hang onto a belief of 2000+ years ago, that the son of mine who was full of Love and Light gave his life for them? They want to hang on to that. What he did do was show them the way, as a Wayshower, a Teacher of profound Truths. However, humanity prefers the distorted version of the Truth. When you are fully in the higher, finer density, you will see more clearly.

If people are having a difficult time visualizing what I mean when I talk about density, go to a garden supply depot and look at the different grains of sand or rock. Some can be very coarse and some can be so fine that it sticks to your hands and you cannot even blow it off—it is so fine. Put the denser one in one hand and the finer one in the other hand. That is what reality is like—the denser and coarser reality, the consciousness like those heavy, coarse grains of sand when you walk on it, versus the fine sand that allows your feet to sink deeply into it, which makes it difficult to walk. The fine sand is the finer density in the higher dimension, in that reality.

I say to you, my dear sons and daughters that **the crucifixion never happened to your Lord Jesus**. He was maligned, told to leave the country. You have a phrase in your Westerns, *get out of Dodge*. In some ways, he was told *get out of Dodge, Jesus, or you will be crucified*. Consequently, he and his wife, Mary Magdalene, left and went into Egypt, as you have been told. My dear children, open your hearts, raise your consciousness, take some deep breaths, pull yourself up by your bootstraps, climb higher, open your minds, let go of all those old belief structures, and let in some new ideas—this idea. It will startle you. It might make you feel somewhat peculiar, but know that is what it feels like when you are letting go of old programming and beliefs. They no longer serve you, as I have said. They will hold you back. You have that saying *time marches on*. Well, beloved children, I hope you just keep marching on with it with open hearts and open minds.

I bless you, for you are My beloved children no matter what color or state of consciousness. I AM with you always.

I AM your Father-Mother God. Adieu.

The Ultimate Experience

JUDAS ISCARIOT SPEAKS

*Good morning my dear one, **I AM Yeshua**. You cannot keep a good man down (smile). As you listen to the wonderful Hebrew prayer on the CD by Barbara Streisand, we hear your gratitude for coming to you to write the book. However, my beloved, it takes two to tango. We want the information out, so that your willingness to do this is equally gratifying to us. This is a shared responsibility, for your Higher Self is very much involved. We all take such joy because of your joy. When one is in service for God, it needs always to be with joy. It is never to be a duty, or drudgery, but it needs always to be approached in joy and happiness. This you do. This you do, my dear one.*

All right, what do we have in store for you today? Today we are bringing in another Being that you have not channeled before and may prove to be quite interesting for you and the Readers. You are already trying to find out who it is going to be. I prefer to let him tell you. Now at least you know it is a male figure, and he was associated with me in those Biblical times. He was one of the Disciples—Apostles—and a trusted friend. Therefore, without further explanation of him, I will let him introduce himself. (Thank you Lord, I am honored.) *The honor is ours.*

Oh my dear Chako, what a privilege this is to speak with you. **I AM Judas.** (*Oh my gosh Lord, I welcome you.*) Not everyone would welcome me so (*laughter*). They would wish that I would hang myself all over again. However, I feel that since this book, this work is from those upper dimensions, it is time for humanity to get the Truth. I have been depicted as betraying the Lord Jesus, as humanity calls him. I will refer to him as *Yeshua*.

He was a dear friend, a childhood friend, and we played together and had amusing games together. I believe he has told you that already. We grew into manhood; he went off on his travels, and I did my education. I became fluent in the Roman language and Greek, so that I could converse very easily with what humanity would call *society*. I was invited to the best social events, by who one today might call the *rich and famous*. I was respected.

Then after a few years, Yeshua returned full of knowledge that I only had read about and wished that I could have known also. We had many chats, as he told me his adventures. He told the stories always with flair, for he was a storyteller, as you know. He always put his little lessons in there, his parables for you to figure out and solve. Many times, I was able to figure them out. On the other hand, I did not know at other times the point he was making. He would have to explain it to me. We had many enjoyable evenings together. He told me that he had been guided by God to put together a group of *Disciples* as he called them—men, actually, for **they** would be accepted as teachers. Women were not that acceptable when it came to teaching males—patriarch societies remember.

There were women of the purist, positive nature who traveled with us. Of course, I am speaking of Mary Magdalene, his wife, Mariam, his sister, and his Mother Mary. She did not come with us all the time, but many times she was with us. The Bible has written that the men who he chose had to give up everything. They had to give up all of their possessions, say goodbye to their wives, and just follow him. Well, beloved Readers, this is another distortion. Why would Yeshua deprive the other men of the solace and intimacy of their wives while he had his confidant in Mary Magdalene? He would not. He realized the importance of the wife to his men. Some of the wives chose to come; others chose to stay home with the children. Those families were often visited by the husband. Therefore, there was **not** this austere *give everything away and follow me,* as the Bible portrays. Again, you can see the hands of the church fathers in this, for in those days, the church fathers were not allowed to marry. Therefore, they were not going to have a group of men who had their wives along. *If I cannot be married, I am not going to let you have your wife either.* The thinking in those days was distorted when the church put out all of these stories to the public. There is so much information that did not happen.

I am speaking through this channel in the high fifth dimension, but I will revisit that third dimension in order to tell you the part I played around that crucifixion. The Bible says that I betrayed my dear friend, Yeshua, by kissing him on the cheek, so the Roman soldiers would know whom to arrest. **That is not true**. That is fabrication. I would never betray a friend, let alone anyone else. I did not do that.

However, I intuitively knew that I would not be with my dear friend very much longer. As I prayed, I communicated with God. Now humanity likes to think that I was such a sinful man betraying their Lord that I did not pray. That is such a distortion of the facts. I was as devout as any man could be in that generation. I prayed. I prayed to God constantly, and He spoke to me through my heart. He told me that my purpose was ending—my purpose to be a helpmate for Yeshua.

When he put together his Apostles, I was the one who handled the money, not because others might be dishonest, but because on an educational level, I knew how to handle money. It was simpler to give the job of being the Treasurer to someone who knew how to do that, than to give it to someone whose skills were in another direction. That did not make me better than they were; it just meant I was using my skills and they were using their skills in a different way.

My purpose was to be with the Disciples for a certain length of time. In that third dimension where Yeshua was crucified, the Romans did come and did bring him before the court. I did not have to point him out. They knew him. Some of their wives would listen to him speak. However, what I did not do was attend those court sessions with him. I did not give him the support, the emotional support that I felt he needed at that time. I did not do that, and I feel sad that I did not.

The Ultimate Experience
JUDAS ISCARIOT SPEAKS

Now as the Bible portrays, since I betrayed the Lord, which I did not, I was in such guilt that I committed suicide. That also is misinformation. **I did not betray him**. I loved him. However, I knew that my purpose for being in a physical body was finished. Therefore, I did take my life. **I had taken my life not out of guilt, but because it was time to end cycle with that lifetime**. Remember, Readers, we have those prebirth agreements. In my agreement on a soul level, I was given permission to terminate that life when I **wished**. Again, the Bible states that suicide is a sin. I suppose that in some circumstances you could think of it that way, for life is precious. If you end it because you do not want to face your enormous problems, in a way you have sinned against yourself. You have then set up a karmic pattern where you will have to come back and face those problems again—probably at a more difficult level. There are circumstances, however, where there is a soul agreement that you can end your life. Be careful, though, for this is very tricky.

If there are any Readers who believe they have reached that state where they can end their life freely, I would caution you greatly, for you could be listening to personality versus Soul. On the other hand, I knew in my heart that I could end my life and I did. I must admit it was not a pleasant death. It took longer than I would have wished, but I soon released from my body. Yes, Readers, I did go to Nirvana; I did not go to Hell, as many believe.

I know there are many Readers who think of me as burning in Hell for what I did to their Lord. Oh, those belief systems are going to get you into trouble one of these days. The previous chapters and Presenters in this book have talked about the third-dimensional reality. In order to set the record straight, **I did not betray Yeshua; I loved him. I did take my own life, not out of guilt, but because I had the permission of my Higher Self to do so.**

Now let us travel up to the fifth dimension where none of the crucifixion had happened. It is always a shock, is it not, when you learn that how you have been programmed for so many years is not true. The crucifixion did not happen. Again, you have the Disciples whom Jesus taught, and I was there as the Treasurer again. However, this time the Roman soldiers came and took the Master to court, then later beat him just enough for him to get the message *you need to leave.* Again, I did not go with him. I was not there. I was not involved, although I knew they had taken him. I found out later what he had been told, for he brought us together and told us. We were shocked and did not know quite what to do with our lives.

I had a choice in this fifth dimension. Was my purpose done and was I to kill myself again, or was I to lead my life in another manner? With much prayer and contemplation, meditation, and fasting, Soul told me that I need not come Home yet if I preferred not to—I could do other things. I could carry on my life. Therefore, I decided to stay a while. I only remained with the Disciples for just a short time, for they were teachers and I was not. I decided to travel. I started traveling to many of the areas of which Yeshua had spoken. I traveled a great deal.

I did not marry, but I did have some pleasing relationships with fine women. You know humanity thinks that every woman needs to be married or she is a prostitute. That is not true. In these higher dimensions, there are fine, pure women who choose not to marry, yet still give their love to a man whom they respect. Now while my relationships did not last for years and years and years, they lasted for a reasonable length of time while I was in a particular country. **I fathered no children**, although I believe there is a book circulating that says I had fathered a child with Mary Magdalene. That is not true. **That is not true!** She was Yeshua's wife. Why would I have relations with Mary Magdalene? I have read that that was because she did not marry Yeshua; therefore, she was free to be with other men. That is not true. It is written that I had a child with her. That is **not** true— certainly not in the fifth reality, nor in the third.

The Ultimate Experience
JUDAS ISCARIOT SPEAKS

There are so many realities and so many theories about people. There is another theory that *when Judas makes the realization about the harm that he did to the Lord and when he admits it, that it will have a repercussion throughout the Universe.* Well, **I did no harm to your Lord**. I think what will have a repercussion throughout the Universe is when people come from that third dimension into those higher planes and realize that I never betrayed him and that I did not take my life because of guilt. However, when you take me off the list of being that evil man who betrayed him, my life would not have any more of a repercussion on the Universe than yours. I was a man who was a Disciple for a while and then traveled. It would be heartwarming for me when people no longer hate me. They have used me as a scapegoat for their own guilt. You see, back in that third dimension when humanity had me betraying Yeshua, it was **their** guilt and they made me their scapegoat. *It was Judas; it was Judas' fault that he was crucified.* They refused to take any responsibility for their thoughts and their actions. Now in the fifth dimension where he was not crucified but instead left the country, people still struggled to carry on their lives, to maintain their lives. There is that saying, *get a life* when someone seems to be stuck in a particular pattern. That is what I did. When my dearest friend, Yeshua, left with his wife, I got a life. I traveled also.

In this fifth-dimension experience I no longer felt that I needed to kill myself when the time came for me to make my transition—when my soul called me Home. I could choose another way. I laid my body down and left it. I just left. It was a swift and pleasant journey.

Therefore, Readers, here I am speaking to you through this channel. I will let you draw your own conclusions whether I was—I will use these terms—*the bad guy or the good guy.* I like to think of myself as being the guy that has heart and is full of Light.

Thank you for listening and letting me be a part of your life for these few pages.

The Ultimate Experience
JUDAS ISCARIOT SPEAKS

I AM Judas.

*My dear sister, I greet you this morning. Let us go back to where we were speaking of Judas. There is much controversy swirling around Judas, as you know. You have read an article put out by Lord Kuthumi that Judas was by my side. It also is written that he did not betray me, for **I had asked him to betray me**. That is a completely different dynamic, is it not? I knew that the energy that we were wishing to transmute needed to have a catalyst. Therefore, I asked Judas to play this role as the protagonist. He was not thoroughly happy with the request, but of course, he accepted his role. Therefore, yes, I did ask him to perform what humanity thinks of as a betrayal.*

The other question is whether Judas died on the cross instead of me. No, Judas did not go to the cross. History has it correct that from a higher choice he hanged himself. I doubt if he will take that way of dying again, but that is what he chose to do (smile).

He was my helpmate, and as you have read, there were three dimensions happening simultaneously. There was the higher dimension of the fifth on up where none of that took place and I was warned by the Sanhedrins and the Roman government to leave the country. That was one dimension. We will call it the higher dimension.

*There was another reality where I went to the cross. This of course, I am refuting, for **it did not happen physically**. Much has been said and Kuthumi was one who said that **this was a holographic physical part of me**. Holographic simply means another reality where you put together a picture of yourself—a walking, talking picture of yourself—and that does the particular deed that you are wishing to accomplish. That complete graphic picture, while receiving the different atrocities played out on it, actually does not feel any of the pain. I did not feel any of that. I knew it was going to be nasty and thereby, I did not make that* *a physical part of me. The other reality was **that I was there physically teaching the Disciples. I was there physically in that lower third dimension, walking that land. That was not holographic**. That was one reality that I was physically walking the land among the people. That was my role—my job description. I loved the people. I came physically and walked that land. That was not holographic.*

*Let us reiterate: There is the **one reality** where I was in the higher dimensions and experienced none of this. There was the **second reality** where I was there physically walking the land. The **third reality** was that I was there holographically, experiencing a crucifixion that was also set up by God and the other players and me in order to transmute the darker energies that the people held at that time. Your Bible talks about how the priests were very unhappy with me. I was a thorn in their side. They did not want to have an Upstart telling them how to interpret the Laws. It never occurred to them that maybe this Upstart was sent by God to bring a new Light for them. However, that was as it was meant to be. The three realities commingled.*

(In Judas' chapter, he said he was not as supportive of you that he now wished he had been. In addition, I had read on the Internet that he was with you at the cross.) *There is some confusion there because my dear friend, Judas, did not accompany me to the courts. He felt that he could have done more. Now here is a question for you, Readers. Was Judas a hologram? Was he physical? What do you think? This channel had not even thought of that until now. You see I could be a hologram and still be talking to a person who is quite physical. I have done that many times. Therefore, Judas was physical. He saw me as being physical also.*

The three different realities became so intermingled. One would have a very difficult time in saying that this happened; that happened; this is true, and that is not true. Humanity put the focus on the hologram, is that not ironic? They killed or thought they killed the man, but it was a hologram and not the actual man. *I certainly was an anomaly to them. Judas was physical. He played the role that I asked him to play. No one need point me out, for people knew me, but he set it up to be a betrayal. I merely asked him to tell the Romans where I would be so that they could come for me.*

All the praying that is reported that I did, I had actually gone into another dimension, so that the person they took was the holographic part of me. It is very easy for me to do. You will be able to do this, Readers, when you are in the upper dimensions and on my side. It is called virtual reality, actually. In your video games, you do this all the time.

I AM Yeshua. *(7-22-06)*

(Lord Kuthumi is channeled by Michelle Manders of SA and His teachings are posted on her website www.info@ palaceofpeace.net.)

The Ultimate Experience

JOHN, THE BELOVED

*Good morning, my dear one **I AM Yeshua**. You have some questions for me this morning.* (Thank you, Lord, and I wish you good morning also. As you know, Judas came in and gave a magnificent four pages of information. Remember in the reading for my book, which I have put in the Appendix, Rowena said there was information that only you wished to give me when the time was correct and not during that reading. Did Judas give out all of the information that you were wanting?) *Yes, dear one, there were points that I definitely wanted him to cover.* (Can you say what those are, please?)

First of all, there is that book by another author that is not accurate. It says that Judas and my Mary had a strong relationship and that he fathered her child. That is not correct. That is not correct in the third dimension nor is it correct in the fifth dimension.

(Judas did not kill himself in the fifth dimension?) *No, no, he did not; he traveled.*

(I do not remember where I read it—might have been in the Matthew Books—that whatever Judas is going to say about his life will affect the Universe. Will you comment on that, please?) *I believe that Judas covered that well. **The impact is that Judas did not betray me and that he did not kill himself over guilt**. All that impaction is caused by humanity's believing in the lower density information. That was not portrayed correctly. Therefore, I am satisfied that the information Judas gave you was what I wanted to come forth. He did not father Mary Magdalene's child; they were friends, but never lovers. I married her. I believe that same book states that I did not marry, for I was not supposed to marry—to mix someone else's DNA with mine. That also is incorrect information. I married Mary Magdalene; we had a very loving, intimate relationship. We had children.*

The Ultimate Experience
JOHN, THE BELOVED

*All right, I think that covers any questions that may have arisen for you from Judas' commentary. Do you feel finished with that? (*Yes, I do, thank you, Lord.) *Now let us move on. Let us bring in some one else whom you have not channeled in the past. Again, it is a male figure and one of my Disciples.* (Hmmm, that sounds intriguing.) *We will let him step forward and let him give you his perspective of what went on in those dimensions. (*Thank you, Lord). *You are welcome, dear one.*

Good morning to you, dear channel, or should I say, Mariam out of my past. I AM **John**, known to many of the religious Readers, as **John, The Beloved**. Actually, we were all the Master's Beloveds. He loved us equally, for as you have been told, he was Love—Love personified in every way.

This book I have been told is bringing in a new revelation to Readers—a revelation that is difficult for many to grasp. I will start back in the lower, dense, third dimension where that Biblical story was actually occurring. I was a Disciple, no more or no less. There is a section in the Bible called the *Books of John*—actually, they are all linked together, *Matthew, Mark, Luke and John*. It is said that I wrote that *Book of John*. Your religious leaders feel that that is the more accurate Book, for I was supposed to have written it a few years after the Lord was crucified. That is not accurate either. While I did put to paper some of the happenings, what you might call keeping a journal, it was very rudimentary. I wrote just little notes here and there, as to what day it was, what the lesson was. Many times the words were not even in a sentence, just a phrase. At that time, it did not occur to me that I would be writing for a Bible that humanity would be studying 2000 years hence. It is just like this book. Will this book still be discussed 2000 years from now? I do not know; I do not know.

Therefore, what is purported to be what I said is other people taking my journal with very crude, rudimentary notations and putting them into sentences that I really did not create. I was merely jotting down a phrase or two, so that I would remember

The Ultimate Experience
JOHN, THE BELOVED

oh that is when he talked about that; or that was the day that he fed the crowd, the day he multiplied the bread and fishes. I did not write something every single day, but just when something happened, that was very unusual. Remember we were still in the third dimension.

The Bible that most of you read has all of us gathered at the last supper where Jesus talks to us and says he will be leaving soon. However, as you have read by now, in the fifth dimension, we did gather and he did talk to us and he did say that he would be leaving soon. In that third dimension, he meant he would be leaving because he would be killed. It is hard for humanity to grasp that the crucifixion needs not to have happened. People in that lower density liked revenge. What is that saying—an *eye for an eye and a tooth for a tooth.* That is the way they lived their lives.

Yeshua would talk about *forgiveness,* to turn away from their enemy, turn their cheek to the other side, but people could not relate to that. They felt that there needed to be some revenge taken on those who were troublemakers. In other words, if you punch me, I will punch you back twice. It would just escalate. The Rabbis were no better in that category, for they too revved up the crowd in order for them to have their vengeance appeased. Many times a Rabbi would slap one of the people who gathered around him to hear his teachings. I believe in your modern times, say fifty years or so ago, the teachers slapped their students. Some used a ruler, while others just used their hands. In the Nunnery, some of those nuns were very cruel people. They would impress upon others their own emotional failings. When they took it out on someone else, it was because inwardly they felt less than the person they were slapping.

When the crucifixion took place in that third-dimensional reality, we Disciples were not as bonded together as one would think. Each reacted in a different way. Some went home to their families; others would come together if they had a best friend in the group. All tried to avoid Roman soldiers. You have read where

The Ultimate Experience
JOHN, THE BELOVED

Peter denied the Lord three times before the cock crowed. Again, that story is suspect, but that would be for him to say. NO.

We were in human bodies so we did fear for our lives. Maybe it was because we knew our lives would end in very difficult ways—most of us would be martyred. Whether the fear was because of what was going on or because we intuitively knew we would be killed, there was fear. We were in human bodies and the bodies were afraid, for most of us died in brutal ways.

Now let us move to the fifth dimension and let us see what happened to the Disciples when there was no crucifixion. The Master taught us. It was almost as if he gave us a crash course on what to teach and how to teach, what to expect. Therefore, after he left, with many tearful goodbyes and hugs, we went through that period of grief. We felt abandoned. We knew he had not abandoned us, and this was the next step for him and his journey in that lifetime, but still we felt abandoned. We felt left behind. However, life goes on. Each of us followed his own path. We taught different people. We taught in small groups. Each of us did his *own thing*, as the saying goes. I enjoyed teaching. I found to my surprise that I was a good teacher. I guess you could say it was because I had heart. I had refined my energies, so I had heart.

I taught many of the parables that we were taught. Since the Master had said them so many times to the different groups that gathered around him, we remembered them. We were able to repeat them and explain them to people. They were simple stories, simple teachings, helping the people to grasp the understanding. We did not have large followings. Great crowds did not come and sit at our feet. We did not have to go and stand on a mount in order for people to see us from a distance. We would just have small groups. What you might call a *class*, just small classes. The students would gravitate to the Disciple to whom they were drawn.

When you think in terms of karma, many of the students would be with one Disciple for karmic reasons. Now they were not thought of as *students*. I am merely using that word to help clarify for you. They were just people who would come to hear what you had to say. Many times, we would teach at someone's house. You would have your supper and then people would gather around and start talking. As I would start talking, they would get quiet and start to ask questions. The stories were then passed around. We helped the people to understand as much as we could. Always keep in mind there were no radios or television, so any news came orally, which was not very accurate either. That was all we knew. Therefore, we taught in that way and carried on the Master's words in that way.

I did love him in the way that a man can love another man—a love of respect and in some cases devotion. Our Lord carried energy; he carried an energy that was so magnificent. He was like a magnet. You were just drawn to him. It was as though we could not get close enough to him. We wanted to reach out and just touch his hand or shoulder, or the edge of his robe. One could almost think of him as a beautiful flower. His energy field was like a beautiful flower. We were the bees that came in for the honey—the Lord's *honey bees*. That was in the third **and** the fifth dimensions.

Now it sounds as if we are just ignoring the fourth dimension. However, when you think in terms of evolution, you do not jump from three to five. You go from the lower third to the upper third, then the lower fourth to the upper fourth, lower fifth to the upper fifth. That is where the author and I are right now, as I am speaking. The many books that are being written and coming out now have a purpose to reach a certain population—a certain energy band of people who are mentally and emotionally in the same energy band.

Let us use music for an example. There are people who listened to music, you know back in the twenties, the flapper music. Then there were the crooners, the lullabies, the songs that had meaningful words. Then the Beattles came forth and changed all of that with a new tempo. The dance changed also. There was the *jitterbugging, the rock and roll.* Now there is what has become known as *hard rock*. However, each of those bands of energy speaks to different people. The hard rockers carry a harder type of energy. It is courser and not particularly refined. There are people who are drawn to that kind of music because it speaks to their energy level versus the softer type of music, the love songs.

Consequently, when you think about music or dancing and how it has evolved from the lower third and is moving forward, it gives you a mental picture as to what is going on in those dimensions. Many people are just finishing the third dimension and moving into the fourth. Those people would still believe the Biblical stories as an actuality. Whereas those people who have refined their energies and have evolved forward on their path cannot listen in an enjoyable way and therefore, simply do not listen to the lower energy music. It ruffles their feathers, so to speak. It ruffles the energy that surrounds them. Therefore, they are drawn to different kinds of music, what some have come to know as New Age music. It is softer, a more angelic sound, perhaps.

Therefore, Readers, you can see evolution in play in your music and in your dancing. In each of those circumstances on the evolutionary path, the energy bands are still separate. They start to converge in the fifth dimension, and when people no longer will buy the CD's with the lower vibration music, then they will no longer be produced. However, I think it will take a generation or two to refine the music once again.

Readers, I have strayed a bit here, but it is my observation that I thought might clarify for you a bit when we jump from the third to the fifth and then back to the third and up to the fifth again in dimensional reality. In the fifth dimension, we did not die those dreadful deaths where some were beheaded, or chained in the dungeons for years, or whatever all those deaths involved. We did not go through that. Just as with Judas, we had a more peaceful choice as to our death.

The Ultimate Experience
JOHN, THE BELOVED

I think I have covered all that needs to be covered at this time. Just know that the crucifixion in the third dimension and the death of many of the Disciples that took place under horrific conditions did not happen in the fifth dimension. The people died a more natural type of death. They were not martyred, for their martyrdoms ended in that higher dimension, that higher reality. The higher realities are closer to God. Why would one come from those ancient beliefs where the mob would burn you at the stake because you would refuse to abandon God and then chose to repeat that in the higher dimension? Now is that not a thought?

With that, I leave you now. Thank you for the privilege of speaking with you.

I AM John.

You *may name this chapter, John, The Beloved. (*Thank you, Lord.*) You are welcome. Adieu.*

The Ultimate Experience

ARCHANGEL MICHAEL

*Dear one, **I AM Yeshua**, back once again. I will say that we are approximately half way through our book. As you have surmised by now, we will be making some changes to the title, but will address that at the end of the book.*

You have a slight imbalance in your throat from your channeling, as you know. Just use some gargle frequently and you will be fine. You can up your vitamin C if you wish, one more tablet to 4000 mg, versus 3000 mg. Your body is quite stable, actually.

Let us go forth with our book. This will not be a four-pager today. It will be somewhat shorter, for the person who is coming forth is coming only to make a few statements. Therefore, I will step aside now and let you hear from one of our angels. You have not had an angel reporting on this book yet, so take a deep breath and get ready to hear his words.

*Good morning, my beloved child, **I AM Archangel Michael**. I came to you the other day during a reading you were giving to a person. I work quite closely with you whether you know it or not, but now you are beginning to know that you can call upon me whenever the need arises.*

When humanity is struggling to advance, to go from one evolution to another, many times the people need help from the more advanced Beings, those that have climbed up Jacob's ladder, mostly from the Archangels. Most people do not realize that they can call upon the Archangels. They may realize that they have angels and guardian angels around them and can call upon those angels. However, they feel that the Archangel is out of their grasp. They think we are royalty and above them. One does not go to royalty and ask for help. That is a fallacy, dear Readers.

The Ultimate Experience
ARCHANGEL MICHAEL

Of course, you can call upon us. You can call upon Archangel Metatron, one of the highest angels there is.

Each of us has an area of expertise. Metatron is associated with Light, electrons and all of that. I am associated with wielding my blue sword. When I wield it, I am severing energies, or cords, or chopping away the debris, so that the soul can walk more easily on its path. People carry so much karmic baggage from one lifetime to another. If they had parents who have chosen the game of *possession*—heavy control—wanting to get rid of it or to experience it again, they bring it from lifetime to lifetime.

After a while, these cords of energies, these bands of energies will hold you back, making it very difficult for you to move forward. That is why so many people have past-life readings. They go to a hypnotherapist, because they have brought from a past-life to this life some energy that is keeping them from doing what they are supposed to be doing in this life. It can be some addiction, some emotional problem that they have brought with them. This is what we call their *karmic baggage*. This is where I can sever those connections, for it does no one any good to keep regurgitating the past—to keep bringing it forward, to keep replaying it. It is done. It is finished. Let it go. I help you sever those ties to your past.

Now one of you, or all of you Readers may be wondering why I am talking about all of this, when the book is about third-dimension reality. It is because when you are in that third dimension reality, you have these lower, dense energies clinging to you. You are attempting to advance yourself, and yet these energies are wrapped up in your different belief systems, which keep you from being able to move forward.

Consequently, that is one of my tasks. I sever those energies and help you to continue. If you are carrying those beliefs that you have learned in previous lifetimes concerning those Biblical stories of the crucifixion and you are still carrying them from lifetime to lifetime, for they did happen 2000 years ago, you need help in letting those go—those lies that were fed you. It is time to let go of that third-dimensional mentality. This is where I come in.

However, I only can help you when you ask. I believe that most of you have heard that you need to ask for your angels' help before they can help. It all stems from the free will that the Creator gave you. We cannot interfere with your free will. Therefore, you just keep coming back repeatedly with the same karmic patterns that could have been severed several lifetimes ago. You need to call upon me. *Archangel Michael, please come and help me to release.* I can be here in a blink of an eye, for I hear your call throughout the Universe. Do not ask me how I do this. I think that this is still a bit beyond most people's understanding (*laughingly said*). It is enough to know that I hear you and I will come.

As you read this chapter, sit and quiet yourself, still yourself. Ask me from the sincerity of your heart to come forth and help **you** sever those past connections. Remember, we do not do the work for you. We help **you** do the work. In other words, it becomes a combined effort with your Soul. You have heard I hope that no one can save you but you; however, some have third dimensional programming that says Jesus will save them. No one saves you but you and that includes me. On the other hand, when people ask for help, then we gladly come swiftly. With your Soul and our energies, we help you. In my case, I sever connections that no longer serve you, that can be negative, dark areas in your life. I help you sever those connections and transmute them.

That is my message for today, dear Readers. This is nothing too profound, but very applicable. It is something that is very simple and easy for you to do. You ask Archangel Michael to come and help you with making that transition from third dimension mentality to the fourth. That is done by transmuting the old energies, by transmuting your belief systems, by severing cords of energy that you are hooked into or that are hooked into you and you no longer need them.

With that, I will leave you now. **I AM Archangel Michael.**

The Ultimate Experience
ARCHANGEL MICHAEL

All right, my dear, this is **Yeshua**. *We thought this information might be helpful for Readers, for we feel there will be many of them wanting to know how they can move forward more quickly—how they can move from the third to the fourth. For many, it is simply a case of asking for help. Many do not realize that they can ask the Archangels for help. This is all for today. Adieu, dear one.*

The Ultimate Experience

ISRAEL-JACOB ben ISAAC

*Good morning, my dearest one, I come to you during the tune of the glorious Hebrew prayer. **I AM Yeshua;** let us go on with our book. It is proceeding nicely, and we are very gratified. All the different Beings that come forth are so happy to be of service. They enjoy it immensely.*

*(*Do I have to raise my energy some more to reach you?*) No, my dear one, it need not even be in your consciousness as to whether you need to rise up or not. You just are there. Do not give it another thought, but just proceed.*

*Now, whom are we going to surprise you Readers with next— whom are we going to present next? You see, Readers, it is just as much of a surprise for you as it is for the author, for she does not know either (smiling). All right, we are going to be bringing in someone from the past, clear back in the past. When I say the past, I am referring to the reality of those Biblical times, to the time of Jacob. (*Oh!*) Are you familiar with the story where Jacob had many sons and they later became the ancestry for the Twelve Tribes of Israel? One of the sons was Joseph. However, as the story goes, Joseph in his youth was a bit arrogant.* (I have noticed in modern times that the male youths are arrogant, also.)

Joseph would take great delight in telling his dreams to the whole family. He would act them out. He would stand up, prance about, and be quite excited—or revved up—during the telling of his dreams. His brothers, who were quite a bit older, ran different levels of jealousy. There is that dynamic where there is rivalry among siblings. One's ego can be more developed than another's. They all had their issues. They decided to get rid of Joseph in some way. The Bible states that story where Joseph was thrown into a pit and rescued when his brothers sold him to a slave-caravan that went on into Egypt. Much of that story is true.

We have been talking in this book so far about different realities. Clear back in Jacob's and Joseph's and his brothers' time, their awareness was not very advanced. They had a second-chakra mentality in the second dimension going into the third. However, Joseph had more awareness. He already was operating in the third dimension. That is why he was able to bring in his dreams so clearly because he had more consciousness than his brothers did.

Many of you may know this, while others may not. Joseph was one of my (Yeshua) past lives. Now why would I, as Joseph-Yeshua have such a lifetime? What was it that I was supposed to do? Remember, this is all by pre-birth agreement. Why would I, as Joseph, agree to be sold as a slave in Egypt? It was to bring the Hebrews into Egypt. When there was the famine all over that area, it was Joseph as the overseer, the second to Pharaoh, who arranged for the granaries to be full so that they could feed their people and others. He then brought Jacob, his brothers and their families into Goshen, Egypt. They had a grand reunion, and thereby escaped the famine. That is all true, for Jacob carried an energy dynamic that they were transmuting which also needed to be brought into Egypt. It was an energy experience set up by God so that the whole Moses story would take place. He would come in and then lead them out again—out of slavery.

This Biblical story, and the reason I am bringing it up, even though it happened in the second and third Reality, was still true. However, the difference that lets this story be true and the crucifixion story not be true in the fifth dimension is that humanity's consciousness was not focused on killing who we would call a "Holy Man." They had their deep religious faith in God plus there was the Goddess energy that was prevalent. Therefore, there was not the evil intent in people's hearts during Jacob's time.

There still were the morals. They were not morally pure, for there was a great deal of sexual activity and drunkenness happening. On the other hand, they were not particularly bent on killing people—Holy people—those who they knew were close to God. They did not kill them. It was in that mentality, the third

The Ultimate Experience
ISRAEL-JACOB BEN ISAAC

dimension at crucifixion time, that people were more into brutal thinking.

The Joseph story has more facets to it. Its main purpose was to get the Jews into Egypt, for there was a great learning experience manifesting. With pre-birth agreements, the souls that came in agreed to be the slaves for Egypt, for there was a mentality that needed to be broken, or a belief system that needed transmuting, for the Hebrews and others did believe in slaves. Many owned slaves who were captives from their wars and skirmishes.

Therefore, there was a slave-mentality there, and they were sent by God into Egypt to break that dynamic. The only way they would ever have gone is the fact that they needed food. The only way they would have gotten food is for Joseph to be sold into slavery. He then experienced all of that—being a slave of Pharaoh, being enticed by a woman and then rising above all of that because he was able to interpret Pharaoh's dreams. All of that is quite accurate. I, Yeshua, was Joseph, the one who had the Coat of Many Colors. The plagues that hit Egypt are another story. It actually is Moses' story, so we will not go further with that. However, I would now like to bring forth Jacob who was called, "Israel."

Greetings to our Readers and to this channel, **I AM Jacob**, the father of all those twelve sons. You know, it is rather amusing, for people today would be quite astonished if they had twelve sons. However, in those days in antiquity, having twelve children was the norm. On the other hand, it was somewhat unusual to have twelve **sons.** I did have a daughter (Dinah), also. As you know, while I attempted to be fair and just, Joseph was an unusual lad, so that I could not help but be very fond of him. I would think that Joseph and your Jesus looked very much the same. They probably carried that same genetic body forward—tall, lithe, quick, and humorous, with a touch of arrogance, which seems to be a trait of youth. Did I leave out handsome? He was a handsome lad, strong and fearless. He had great courage and a great heart.

The Ultimate Experience
ISRAEL-JACOB BEN ISAAC

Joseph also never could quite understand his brothers. He could not understand the fuss they would make, except he knew they were jealous of him. However, he also felt *what's your problem? What's your problem,* he thought as he would tell them his latest dream that happened to have a way of always coming true. This would drive his brothers to distraction, for they knew he was right and this would just—to use your expression—bug them. However, I was as fair and just with them as I possibly could be. I loved them. They were my children.

I talked to God. I talked to Him with my heart so that when I died, I felt little difference between God and me. I felt as if there were no separation. He told me to do something; I would do it. I knew how important it was when I laid my hands on the head of each of my sons and gave them my blessing, for I knew that whatever I said would come to pass. Your Bibles tell my words quite accurately—not entirely, but quite accurately. I knew their traits; I knew their fallacies; I knew their truths; I knew their hearts. I knew them, for they were my sons. I knew Joseph for the Light that he was. Joseph had two wonderful sons himself. He had more children, but the first two sons were the ones whose ancestry became the two Tribes, *Manasseh and Ephraim,** of Israel. Those sons I blessed and gave them the prophecy that all came to pass. You can read that in your Bibles, also.

When we went into Egypt and saw the splendor that my son, Joseph, was living in, it astounded us, for we led simple lives. We were like nomads, living on the land with our flocks of sheep and goats, and traveling from one oasis to another. We were never without something to eat, but when those hard years came, I knew in my heart that we had to go to Egypt and ask for grain. At first, I did not trust the man who no longer was called Joseph (*Zaph'nath-pa-a-ne'-ah*), for I did not know who he was. I knew he had an Egyptian wife (*Asenath, daughter of the High Priest Po-tiphe'-rah of On*). That fact helped shield from me that he was my son. It never occurred to me that one of my sons would marry an Egyptian woman. Consequently, it was a shock to meet Joseph and his family. His wife was very beautiful, had a loving heart, and loved Joseph and her children.

His sons were handsome lads. One was more serious than the other was. Manasseh was the jovial one. He did not take life too seriously. On the other hand, Ephraim was more reserved and a thinker. He did not talk spontaneously, but when he said something, you found yourself listening, for he spoke Truth. He carried a great peace in his heart.

I died an old man, as the Bible says. I blessed them all. I blessed Joseph, for I knew then that he was destined for great things—not only in that lifetime, but in future lives. He was destined for greatness. I did not know at the time that my sons would be the heads of the Twelve Tribes of Israel. Some writers just clump Manasseh and the Ephraim Tribes as one and call them the *Joseph* Tribe. Nevertheless, the Ephraim Tribe was a strong tribe. Joshua came from the Ephraim Tribe. Joshua was Jesus, so you have Joseph as Jesus, and Joshua as Jesus. This author was involved also, but that information as to who she was will remain hidden for now.* Suffice to know that she played a role with Joseph in Egypt, also.

The purpose of my coming this morning for this book is to help clarify information concerning those different dimensions, the second and third dimensions, those realities. Many of the stories are true, for even the crucifixion happened in that third dimension. If you go to the fifth dimension where many of us are, I can say that the Joseph story still happened, for that energy transference had to manifest. It was for the evolution of the Hebrews to get them out of the slave mentality and to put freedom in their hearts. In the fifth dimension with the Hebrews going into Egypt, that is true. Therefore, you see that **not everything that happened in one dimension is negated**. If there is a purpose for changing an energy band for humanity, then it happens.

However, when humanity sinks so low as to want to kill a Holy Man—Jesus—then that same mentality is not carried forward and did not happen in the fifth dimension. You may be thinking *what about all the wars in those Biblical times?* Did God order Joshua to go in and kill thousands in order to clear that land for the tribes? What do you think, Readers? What do you think? That was humanity's mentality of a ferocious God—a God that would order Abraham to kill his son, Isaac, as a test. God would not do that. In the fifth dimension, that did not happen. Therefore, not all of those savage killings of thousands and thousands by Joshua and others were carried forward. That was humanity's consciousness at that time—that God ordered all of this to happen. It does not happen in the fifth reality.

Dear friends I hope there has been some clarification for you. The different realities are such a complex situation. Is Jacob still alive? Well, he is not in a body, but he definitely is alive. He is with the Heavenly Host or the Company of Heaven, or however you wish to put it. Of course, Joseph, Yeshua, and I, Jacob-Israel, would still be connected, for we had great history together—great history.

It has been my honor and privilege to come to you. I bless each one of you, as I blessed my sons. May God keep you and may your purposes be accomplished, so that you can arrive in Nirvana knowing you have done well with your lifetime. There is that saying that many Christians are hoping Jesus will say to them when they arrive, *well-done, good, and faithful servant.* Well, I would not think of myself as a servant. I am in service to God, but that does not make me His servant. It makes me part of His family, part of Him, or one could say a *partner in life.* I leave you now.

I AM Jacob, or better known as ***Israel.***

(Is there anything else that you would like to add to this, Master?) *No, dear one, for when you type this up, you will see that it is sufficient. So until tomorrow, I AM **Yeshua**.*

The Ultimate Experience
ISRAEL-JACOB BEN ISAAC

(Author: Note that Joseph went up into Egypt as a slave. He was bought by **Potaphar, the Captain of the Guards** *for Pharaoh, and remained in that position for seven years. Joseph later was brought before Pharaoh in order to interpret Pharaoh's prophetic dreams. Joseph interpreted the dreams correctly, thereby Pharaoh gave* **Joseph an Egyptian name, Zaph'-nath-pa-a-ne'-ah**, *and promoted him to be Governor of all Egypt, second only to Pharaoh. He also gave him as wife,* **Asenath**, *the daughter of the* **High Priest, Po-tiphe'-rah of On**. *History only records* **two sons, Manasseh and Ephraim,** *although we are led to believe there were more children.*

Joseph lived and experienced slavery, transmuted it, and lived in freedom until he **died at one hundred and ten years of age.** *He was embalmed. His bones were later carried out of Egypt by Moses when he liberated the Hebrews. Joseph's bones were transported for forty years until he was carried finally to his resting place in Israel. It is not known whether Manasseh and Ephraim's bones were carried into Israel or remained in Egypt.)*

*(Ephraim was one of the author's past lives.)

The Ultimate Experience

JOSEPH of THE COAT of MANY COLORS

*(***Yeshua** and I had a discussion about the content of our book versus others he has co-authored, mainly Glenda Green's book, Love Without End, 1999). Her book is of a different nature. It was for her to use as a teaching tool, since she has that strong intellectual background that just brought in that aspect of me for her books. Her books are for a teaching tool. Our books with you are not what we would call," teaching books." They are books to spark one—to get a person thinking about his or her own belief systems. Are they able to let that old belief go?*

Therefore, we have introduced this new information in a gentle way. We repeat frequently, for we are working with the body. When people read a book, they read it from a soul level, from a personality level, from an ego level, which is the body level. Consequently, we are providing these different levels for the different levels of that person. It is hoped that by the end of the book they will start seeing that there is a new way of looking at history.

I have told you in the past that I am a history buff. History is ongoing. It is a continuous movement. Since it is continuous, it all depends on what segment of that continuum you visit. Are you going to visit the segment of the crucifixion? Are you going to visit the segment of Jacob's and Joseph' time? Are you going to visit the segments of World War II, or Viet Nam, or up to the present—the Bush administration? That is history, also. All this is happening on a continuum. It is history.

If you travel far enough on the continuum, then we are speaking with you and we are making a book together in the fifth dimension. The fifth dimension is touching, actually, the sixth dimension. It is all on a continuum. What you see today will not be what you see tomorrow. Therefore, one needs to change and keep changing one's belief systems, for people are too apt to bring toward them a belief and then hold on to that belief and

*never let it change in any way. This is similar to the Christians'
belief that Jesus is the same today as he was yesterday and will
be tomorrow. That is an erroneous belief system that Christians
hang on to and refuse to change.*

*When someone takes on a belief system, strange as it may
seem, it is a particular belief with which the person resonates.
He likes the idea that Jesus is going to stay absolutely the same.
Therefore, if he never changes, then in some way they can trust
that "he will always stay the same and never change and that way
I will know he always will love me." Beliefs are so intermingled
with people's own egos and morals. There is no room then to
bring new information into their thought processes.*

*Therefore, with this fourth book—and you know there will
be a fifth and sixth book, but one at a time (smile)—here in this
particular book, we repeat ourselves. We repeat to help the souls
awaken. We repeat so that the personality gets it. We repeat so
the body can let go of its ego wanting to hang on to its erroneous
thought—maybe a cruel thought. There are still people who do
not realize that thoughts are energy. And that everything they
think has energy. Consequently, if they are thinking wrongly
toward someone, that energy goes to that person. Many do not
know this. They do not even understand the concept. That is what
we would call the third-dimensional mentality—not having the
awareness to think beyond the box, shall we say.*

*Their awareness has not increased. Consequently, their
boundaries have not broadened either. I am thinking of an
example: Pour a glass of water on a tabletop. It moves out for
a while and then stops, for there is nothing that helps it to move
further. People's consciousness is similar to a glass of water that
you spill on the table or on the floor. The water moves just so far
and then it stops until it has another glass of water spilled on top
of that and then it travels some more. People's consciousness and
awareness react in the same way. They need some dynamic that
will keep moving it forward.*

The Ultimate Experience
JOSEPH OF THE COAT OF MANY COLORS

Many times the soul brings in grief, for we have found that grief helps a body to move forward in consciousness. It is painful, but does get one out of a rut in order to have new ideas. Many times people in grief have never thought of joining a group. However, with a death in the family, they may find that they join a grief group. That is a new experience for them. That is moving them forward. Alternatively, there could be the grief from a long illness and the caregivers are learning something new—what it is like to take care of someone and to give of themselves. Maybe they have never done this before.

Thereby, usually something dynamic or traumatic helps move a person forward in consciousness. If someone were having a very happy life, many times that person needs a shove to go onward and not just keep treading in the same spot and enjoying themselves—not giving to others, perhaps.

Therefore, to you Readers, in this Book FOUR, we have brought in many speakers and each one is adding just a small segment to the mix. Now you who are more intellectual may think there is not enough meat; you need more of a hearty meal here than you are receiving in this book. However, we are doing this on purpose because if it were a hearty meal you were enjoying, you might not get past the first chapter or so.

Mariam started the book off in a delightful, child-like way, talking about the bug fort that we used to build. She then went on to tell how Benjamin was healed. Then the tone changed for the book somewhat. We started bringing in different Beings such as Archangel Michael—shifting, you see, always shifting. Now we have just brought in Jacob, and the book shifted again to show you the different dimensional levels. We picked out stories that you would know. Not everyone has read the Bible...

(Author: It was at this point that I lost contact due to my tape recorder malfunction. None of Joseph's segment was recorded during this sitting.)

The Ultimate Experience
JOSEPH OF THE COAT OF MANY COLORS

Hello my precious one, **I AM Yeshua**. *We had a bit of a problem with the tape recorder yesterday, did we not?* (Yes, I am so sorry. I did not tape anything of what Joseph was saying.) *Never mind, we will bring him forth again in a few minutes.* (I did not record the rest of your thoughts either, as to what you were saying.) *Well, let us pick up from there then.*

All right, let us continue. We had described how we had set up this book. Yes, we have it shifting a bit with each chapter. In that way, it retains the attention of the Readers. We do not want them to get bored through this process, you see (smile). (I don't think so.) *As we shifted, we would bring in another Presenter. The energy from that Presenter would help shift the Readers' belief systems a bit—always with the purpose in mind that we are helping them to shift those beliefs. We brought in Jacob and that more or less introduced the subject of the Hebrews transmuting their slave mentality. We had spoken how that slave mentality came all the way into present time. Even in the pilgrims' day of the 1700's that was presented on television, when the pilgrims captured Indians, they sold them as slaves and sent them out of the country. Therefore, there was that slave mentality that it was all right to own slaves—then America had its Civil War that broke up the slave mentality in the third dimension.*

Let us continue with Joseph since this is his chapter. Let me bring him forth so that he may speak once again. (I am sorry. The tape recorder was low in batteries and I did not catch it in time. I accept responsibility and do apologize.) *Dear one, there is no problem here with us (smile). You are working with a machine that can malfunction every once in a while and you do not always know the reason for it. All right, let us continue. I will step aside and we will let Joseph of the Coat of Many Colors step forth—one of* **my** *past lives. I must admit that I did enjoy that lifetime once I got past the trials and tribulations of being a slave. You see, I too was a Hebrew and carried those genes that all Hebrews*

*carried at that time, that it was all right to own slaves. All right,
I will step aside now.*

Good morning to the author and the Readers of this book.
I am privileged to come once again. **I AM Joseph.** You know
me as ***Joseph of the Coat of Many Colors.*** The women wove a
magnificent coat for me—a coat that held much energy. All of
the different colors, using dyes that were available to them at
that time, represented the Rays. It was a very colorful coat and a
potent coat full of energy.

I believe I was telling you that this was a pre-birth agreement,
and I enacted the part that was given to me. My brothers put me
into this pit. Some hoped I would die and others did not want any
part of it, but they still left me there. The purpose was to sell me
to a slave caravan that was approaching. They then sold me as
a slave, covered my coat with blood and took it home to Jacob
with the lie that I had been killed by a wild beast. All of this was
pre-arranged and all was true. In the meantime, I then had the
experience—the Soul wanted the experience—of being a slave.

Consequently, that put me in with other slaves, and I was able
to talk to them, to be part of their experience, and to rely upon
God to help me rise above it. So many of my fellow slaves did
not have the belief in the one God, for they believed in idols and
their particular gods. Thereby, many of them had a more difficult
time than I did. Again, everything was pre-arranged before we
were born. I was bought by Potaphar, the Captain of the Guards
of Pharaoh. He treated me decently, but still treated me as a
slave, for that was what I was. However, he saw that I was able to
reason and use my mind, as an educated man would, so that their
fields, gardens, and animals flourished, thanks to the blessings
and Grace of God.

Potaphar's wife played her part in alluring and enticing me. I
had to rise above that, for Potaphar was kind to me and I would
never betray him by sleeping with his wife. That whole story is
in the Bible. Most of it is true. He did not want to kill me, so he

99

did the only thing that he could do—he put me in the dungeon with the other men who were of a more brutal mentality. I was beaten. I learned not to speak unless I was spoken to first. One learns a great deal when one is a slave. All of this was a learning experience for the Soul. I do not need to repeat the whole story, for the Bible tells you this. Eventually I was brought before Pharaoh, interpreted his dreams and he then raised me to be Governor of Egypt, second only to him. He gave me a beautiful wife, Asenath; she gave me my sons, Manasseh and Ephraim, and I had more. I also had a daughter.

Life, actually, was good then. I was happy. I worked hard. I saw the fruits of my labor. However, there was pain in my heart, for I missed my father. I knew he was greatly pained when my brothers told him that I had been killed. Eventually, my brothers had to come for grain, and eventually, my father had to come, also. It was a wonderful reunion. Life went on. My father, Jacob, became frail, and eventually died. I too, reached the ripe old age of one hundred and ten and then I died.

Now what do these entire narrations have to do with the third dimension or this book? It is to show you that **not** everything in the Bible is to be negated, nor is everything in the third dimension negated and not continued into the fifth. It is a continuum. Let me see if I can give you an example. You know when stage directors are directing a play, many times they are not sure how it should end. The writers will write one ending; they stage that. They then write another ending and stage that. If there were a curtain between the two plays that were going on at the same time, the viewer could see both endings happening. Therefore, we could see the crucifixion playing on one side of the curtain and on the other side there would be no crucifixion.

Alternatively, my life as Joseph was on one side of the curtain and on the other side the Director decided to carry forward the same play to a different ending. But the Director of this play was God. The play needed to be brought forward, but the crucifixion never came from God. That was from humanity's thought forms, not from God. The Christians, however, passed it down as being from God. They took everything in that story and made it symbolic mixed with their own reasoning as to the cause of this or that. Everything meant something—the falling while carrying the cross, the *Stations of the Cross*, Jesus' words, his last words—all of that was invented. The interpretation of what he said was not true, but they **thought** that was what they heard him say. Remember, that was on one side of the curtain and on the other side, which was the fifth dimension, that was never there at all. That play never happened. However, with the Joseph story, God was directing the play, and the Hebrews were transmuting energies so that they could then proceed with the next phase of the play. Moses would then deliver them, bringing them out of Egypt. They were no longer slaves. That dynamic was broken. They then had other experiences where they learned to trust.

This book touches just a small portion of the Truth, but unless people are willing to let go of their belief systems so that new ideas can come forth, they can proceed no further. Thereby, they are no longer hearing Truth. That is the purpose of this book. That is the purpose of the different Presenters coming in. My purpose, as Joseph, is to give the Readers a different idea. Think of it as watching a play and the curtain is the dividing factor between the different dimensions. Therefore, on one side of the curtain, the play happened and on the other side, it may not have happened. Alternatively, on one side of the curtain, the play happened and on the other side, it also happened. It always depends on who is orchestrating the play. If it is God, it goes forward. If it is humanity, it does not, unless humanity does not move forward either so that on that continuum in history humanity is still playing out its evil, its darkness.

I think that is all I need to say. Thank you, Readers, and stay tuned, for there is more to come.

I AM Joseph.

THE INFORMATION CONTINUES...

*This morning we are not going to bring in a particular person, but a blend of all of us. We are greeting you as your **Brothers in Christ**, for we wish to give you more information. This will be a chapter in itself. The purpose of this is to keep clarifying the information, for as you were saying to friends, "When the author is confused, the Readers will be confused also." Let us pick out some of the questions that are roaming around in your mind.*

One of them is—we will use the crucifixion as the example— you are again asking if the crucifixion happened per se in the third dimension. We will say YES, in that third dimension, for that was the people's reality. In her book, Anna washed my body, and that was **her** reality. You have heard many times that everything on Earth is an illusion—different people's illusions. In your present day when terrorists blew up trains in India, you cannot say that that did not happen, for it did, and hundreds of people were killed. However, on the continuum in a different dimension, it did not, for in a different dimension there are no terrorists. There is Love.

Let us go back to the lower third dimension, where the crucifixion happened in some people's perception. If you, the author, were there, but in the fifth dimension, none of this would have taken place. I know; you are still confused. That is why people have a difficult time in releasing these beliefs, for these illusions are so ingrained that they see them as a reality—that it actually happened and became a present reality, but it did not. For now, we will reiterate this for those people, humanity, in the lower third dimension, the crucifixion did happen. (*Let me ask this, for the actual players of the play, it happened? Judas betrayed you, etcetera?*) That happened in some people's perceptions, in some people's illusions. However, the Truth is that I left; I was not there. Still confused? (*Yep.*)

I believe that much of the confusion lies in the fact that it is difficult for people to realize that there could be two different things happening at the same time. There could be two worlds. In one world, this is happening. In another world, that is happening. However, you see, that is an illusion also that there are two worlds. There are only dimensions. Let us proceed further here.

In days of old, people believed in many myths. There were myths about the prehistoric creatures that roamed the Earth. There were myths about the centaurs, half goat and half man. There were myths about mermaids. Now who is to say that any of that mythology was not true? That is when humanity was playing at creating its **own** forms. When they did not know what they were doing, they made mistakes. Or they did it on purpose to experience the results. As a result, you would have half creature—half man or woman. That was a reality. Consequently, you could say that mythology was a reality, one reality—the lower denser reality. Now come to present time. What is the reality of this world or of this history that you are living? Were the India train explosions a reality? Yes, they were. You see when the illusions become so physical, it no longer is an illusion. It did happen, brought about by a group of terrorists with dark thinking, terrorists who have gone towards the dark, versus the Light. Their souls are not dark. It is the personality, the body that has lost touch with the Light within them, which would be their soul. Therefore, the India present-day tragedy is real. Again, one cannot judge this, for these circumstances were pre-birth agreements. All of the people in that play had the pre-birth agreement from the terrorists to the people who were injured or killed. However, even though this is in present time that does not mean that it is happening in a higher dimension. It is still in the lower dimensions. People who have those kinds of pre-birth agreements are in the third dimension, using their free will.

Now you who are in the fifth dimension, which also includes this author, would not see this happening, for that would not be your reality. (*That does not make sense to me, for I saw it on TV, and I am in the fifth dimension.)* When you are on our side, and in the fifth and sixth dimension, that does not happen—that reality does **not** happen. It would be an illusion. We spoke yesterday of history and the continuum. We told you how you could visit segments of history on the continuum. The segment that happened with the train explosions in India is in the past, but still in the third dimension. On the continuum, that cannot happen. Those are humanity's thought forms.

I know this is confusing to people. Many times people will sign on for a part in a destructive play because it helps propel them into a new reality. One must have one experience from which to build another experience. Those types of disasters that you have chosen to be a player in always have a purpose, you see. They are another stepping-stone, from which you can step further toward something else, always forward.

I know in the Matthew Books in the chapter *Jesus*, God said that the crucifixion did not happen, and that Jesus was sent out of the country. That is Truth. However, since plays are always ongoing, you can tap into different people's realities. Therefore, when Anna, the Grandmother of Jesus, dictated her material to Claire Heartsong for her magnificent book, she wrote of that crucifixion, for that was a very real reality for her.

As you know, this author was there as Mariam and was part of that drama at that time in Anna's reality. However, another aspect of Mariam said *goodbye* to Yeshua and his family as they fled the country, for that aspect did not carry the perception that Yeshua went to the cross. You have these different realities going on that very aware Souls can check the Akashic records, can tap into these different realities, and see what is happening in the world. **There are layers and layers of different realities, all ongoing, just as there are layers and layers of dimensions**. In that third dimension, there are many layers of realities. One of the most dominant ones is the crucifixion. There also are other realities where Judas never betrayed Yeshua.

I hope this has added another segment for you Readers to help clarify all of this. It is not an easy concept. If you had the ability to astral travel, you could travel to these different realities, but you would need a master guide with you, for it could be quite dangerous. Parts of yourself could be left behind—stuck in those realities. Your present personality would become very confused. We feel that astral travel is not for the average person, but for the adept, the master in embodiment who knows what he or she is doing.

We will close on that note, that there are many realities—not just one—but many realities in the many dimensions. Said another way, there are many realities in **the** third dimension. Some are carried forward and others are not, for it is all an illusion. Illusions are only made manifest by humanity's thought forms. If enough people believe in an illusion, it becomes more solid; it becomes the probability. It happens, for that would be you joining others in the same reality in the same play. With that our dear Readers, we will bring in others tomorrow. We are your **Brothers in Christ.**

The Ultimate Experience

PLATO, THE PHILOSOPHER

*Good morning, to my dear soul and author of my heart, you are doing quite well. Let us talk about today's work. This book is approximately half finished. In the first half of the book, we brought various Beings forward so that you Readers might remember and associate different stories with them. Our purpose was for each Presenter to give just a little snippet of information, so that perhaps you would be able to hear the Truth more and to let go of some of those belief systems that you hold onto so dearly—let the untruths fall to the wayside. As we have said before, dear Readers, much that you have been taught by well-meaning parents and religious teachers is not necessarily true. It is **their** truth, you see, and not true spirituality.*

Therefore, we are hoping to bring some of that Truth to you, for the biggest hurdle for you to overcome is believing that everything you have read, everything that you have heard no matter what it is, is not necessarily Truth. In present day, you have your television and your newspapers. They are not necessarily Truth, for as you know, many times in your government, the Truth is not spoken. The lies are given to the public for the purpose of the liar's own desires. If a person harbors a particular desire, a particular way of presenting him or herself, then that person will put out a story that is not necessarily true. It may have a little tad of truth in it, but will not necessarily be all true. There is that saying "an ounce of Truth and a pound of lies." I am afraid that becomes more of a Truth for you, as far as the politicians, newspapers and television reporters are concerned.

You realize that the Bible is no different. The church fathers took the scriptures out of context and since they could not remember themselves what I, Yeshua, had said, they distorted the words with what came from their own consciousness, their own illusions of what had happened. Keep in mind that much of what I supposedly had said in my Teachings was being remembered

106

The Ultimate Experience
PLATO, THE PHILOSOPHER

thirty plus years afterwards—after the fact. Not many of you can repeat what was said after the fact the next day from a phone conversation, let alone thirty years later and report that this is what he or she said. It is ridiculous.

However, the church fathers of long ago would repeat these lies, these illusions, and their own concepts over and over. They would have people memorize them, so that soon it sounded like Truth to the people. Not many of the people were that educated. They learned by rote, by repetition. It made no difference to them, for they did not know that maybe the person was not all that objective, but had just interpreted these different passages through his own ego.

For today's work, I am going to bring in an old philosopher, for in his day, he too was giving the world new ideas. Now was he totally correct in the way he saw the world? No, not totally, but he gave people a new way to look at things. Without further words from me, I will step aside and let the next speaker introduce himself.

To you Readers, **I AM Plato, The Philosopher.** I come from the ancient past, for I was one of the first philosophers who offered a different view of the world—a world where people shared with each other. It was more of a Utopian type of world, but it gave people a new way of looking at life. One could say that my Platonic view of the world was an illusion, a particular reality, and it was. It was my reality where people of different cultures would come together, serve each other, and love each other. I worked out intricate steps, or diagrams, if you will, for the ideal world—the Platonic view of the world. I did practice what I preached, and people thought I was quite peculiar, for my head was very much in the clouds. I was pulling information to me from the Universal Mind. I was pulling to me a different reality from what people were familiar with.

I doubt if uneducated people even had heard of me, for during those times, hundreds of years ago *(Webster, circa 427?-347?*

107

BC), there was such a demarcation between the wealthy and the poor. The wealthy had education. The poor did not. The wealthy had jewels and magnificent homes. The poor did not. The wealthy had six-course meals. There was such a waste of food that the servants made money feeding the beggars, selling a piece of bread for a coin or two. Therefore, the beggars, the thieves, those who were just trying to stay alive, could care less about my Utopian view of life.

I decided I would see if I could reach the mind, the awareness of any of those urchins. I noticed one lad who was quite desperately trying to stay alive. He would cover himself with papers, huddle next to different people's fires to stay warm, and eat garbage that was thrown outdoors, but I could feel something about him. There was a mind lurking under all that filth. I had my servant bring him to my house. I had the servant strip him of his clothes, wash him, feed him, then give him a bed to sleep in.

The next day I had the lad brought to me. He cowered in front of me and showed a bit of arrogance to questions that I asked him, but the arrogance was to cover up his fear. When someone like me takes another person from his environment, he becomes afraid, for there are no realities to cling to—to help stabilize him. In other words, if I had had something from his world that he could have leaned against, that would have given him a sense of stability. However, here was a lad who had never walked on carpets, never had been in a house that was lit, never had anything more to eat than someone else's leftovers, never had his own clothes to wear. Now he was standing in front of me as something to be feared, for you see that mentality had him feel that nothing good could ever happen to him.

He expected punishment or something unsavory if anyone were kind to him. I wanted to prove my theory that there was kindness in people. I did not speak to him for very long. I offered him a seat and asked him if he would consider staying with me for a while. Of course, he immediately wanted to know why. Did I want him to steal something for me? Did I want him to procure something for me that I was not able to do myself? When I answered, *No, I want to teach you, for I see something in you that others do not see, nor do you see yourself.* **I see that you have a soul, and you do not even know what that is.**

The lad was not stupid. In a cunning way he knew a good thing when he was given one. Consequently, he agreed. I assigned a servant boy to be his companion. The boy was just a few years older and had been with me for quite a while. He knew my ways. He knew what I was attempting to do. Therefore, he stayed with the lad, slept in the same room in different cots, ate together in the servants' quarters. You see, one does not immediately bring someone from the street into your parlor and into your dining room with all the silver goblets simply because the person would not be able to handle what he would think was the richness of all of this. Therefore, we must raise a person up gradually, keep him clean, and give him clothes, not opulent but good clean clothes that a working person would have, and feed him several times per day, for he was a growing lad. He had the run of those servants' quarters, also. I then got him a tutor and started his lessons. At first there was only about an hour of studies, maybe in the morning and then again in the afternoon. I then increased it until he was studying several hours a day. To my delight, he was like a sponge and just filled himself with all of these new ideas and information. Now I grant you that clear back in my day, we did not have the inventions that you do now, Readers. We did not have the knowledge that you do now, Readers. You would think of us as being quite antiquated. I guess we were, as you will be some day when someone looks back at the year 2006 when humanity is in the year 3006. How ancient you will think that generation was.

Now as I have said, the purpose for bringing the lad into my home was to lift him up and out of his born station in life and raise him to new levels. I wanted to see if he could adapt. Did he have that inner awareness to adapt? Could his body keep moving forward, for his soul certainly was delighted? I also realized that this was just one lad, one experiment in a person's life. I did not play this out to harm the boy in any way, for I realized he was my responsibility. Once you raise a person up, you do not just dump him back into his old way of life—of garbage and rags. You have a responsibility now. You have in essence created a new Being who will become part of your family. Therefore, I provided for him; I taught him; I saw that he married a woman with good morals. They had children. I saw that he was employed, and he was a happy man and lived a long life.

In that experiment, I wanted to know if someone who was born into one reality could adapt into another reality. Since this book is on realities, do you not see where those two realities—one of the poor and down trodden and one of the more blessed and well-fed—are parallel but never meet because one is afraid to cross over to the other? The other one is loathed to fall back into the lower level.

Now if you in your astral travels went to my reality and visited me, you would see the life that I lived, the prosperous life. Since there are no beggars on my street, if you came with no predetermined ideas, you would not know that there was another reality a mile or so away from me. What I am bringing to your attention, Readers—since it is mainly the crucifixion that we are dealing with—is that the crucifixion happened for some and for others it did not.

In your present-day life when you work your jobs, have your entertainment, listen to your music, watch your movies and television, know that there is that reality and for others there is none of that. It is not **in** their reality. However, that other reality is still ongoing, is it not? In my philosophy of the Utopist way of life, in some ways everything was wishful thinking. I was merely bringing the concept into written words on how life could be. I was pulling from the Universal Mind. I did not know that at that time, but I was writing how life could be—the Utopist way of living—Plato's Utopia (the elitist state).

The Ultimate Experience
PLATO, THE PHILOSOPHER

Down throughout the years, I have been other personages, but probably none as well known as that lifetime. It may interest you to know that that idealism could still be viable, but it is not too likely, for that is a vision for people in the higher dimensions. Now there are some populations in other worlds, in other Universes, that are Utopist in the way that they approach life. It is an interesting fact that whenever a person reads or hears of a new idea, it is only new because it is being heard for the first time. There really is nothing new, for God has created all. It has already been created. It is waiting only for humankind to tap into it and bring it forth. Your wonderful Masters of music, your Mozarts, your Beethovens, your Bachs, each had a way of tapping into the Angelic Realm and bringing that music forth. It is all there waiting for you. The Utopist world is even there. When you read how your wars are instigated by excessive wants of someone else's resources, or are driven by perverted egos, one wonders why a person cannot tap into the higher realms. Why must people have more of what they already have? I know, it is called *greed*. However, philosophers always want to know *why* and I am still a philosopher at heart.

My dear Readers, my purpose was to give you a glimpse of a different realilty that took place clear back in my time. Know that there are many realities within the dimensions. With that I leave you now, and I thank you for the privilege of being asked to come to speak to you, for it has been many an eon since I have spoken to people to give them my views. Thank you, for I am greatly honored.

I AM Plato, The Philosopher.

(Is there anything you wish to add to this, Yeshua?) *No, dear one, we thought that having a philosopher on board would be quite a nice change. 'Til tomorrow, beloved, **I AM Yeshua**.*

(Note: The Internet provides much information on Plato, the Greek philosopher. I have taken the following quote from www.spaceandmotion.com/Philosophy-Plato-Philosopher.

The Ultimate Experience
PLATO, THE PHILOSOPHER

htm. Scroll to Greek Philosophy: *Plato the Philosopher...Truth Reality of Plato* . . . He was a pupil of Socrates and a teacher for Aristotle*).*

Plato Education Quotes... for the object of education is to teach us beauty.

And once we have given our community a good start, the process will be cumulative. By maintaining a sound system of education you practice citizens of good character, and citizens of sound character, with the advantage of a good education, produce in turn children better than themselves and better able to produce still better children in their turn, as can be seen with animals (Plato, 380BC).

*(*Note: I felt that the above quote was a definitive description of what Plato's purpose was when he brought the lad off the street and educated him, as told in our story.)

The Ultimate Experience

THE GODDESS ATHENA

Good morning, my precious one, **I AM Yeshua**. *I come to you this morning with sadness in my heart with what is going on in the whole Middle East area—all those blessed people of God, so frightened, not able to trust each other. They think that the only solution is to kill each other. It makes us very sad. It will play itself out. America will fumble around, not receiving good advice, and President Bush does not know what to do. God shines His Light and Love over all. Many people are praying for all the parties involved.*

It is all part of the changes. As you know, the dark must surface so that the Light can transmute it. It is part of the continuum. It also is what one could call God's Methodology, for the hatred in people's hearts—those who harbor hatred versus peace—must manifest so that it can be transmuted. Thereby, awareness and Light can come to the dark areas. It will happen. There will be a type of truce, but not for a while, not before many more are killed. Let us leave that sad situation for now and focus on our book.

We are delighted with our philosopher-friend Plato's story. As he says, "once a philosopher, always a philosopher." It was quite delightful. Now what do we have in store for you today? I am sure you can hardly wait. (Yes, so what do you have up that spiritual sleeve of yours, my Lord?) *Well, what we are going to do is reach clear back again into history. It is so amusing and fun for us to bring several of these old souls forward, these Ancients from the past, to let them speak their piece. One could almost say they are lined up in back of me, almost shoving the other one out of the way (laughing). They are exclaiming, "Can I go next? Can I go next?" (Laughing) It is rather amusing. Consequently, for today, I will again step aside and let the next one speak. This time we are bringing a woman forth, for as you know, I practiced equality among women. We do not want this book to be too heavy*

113

with male energy. Therefore, let us bring in more of the female energy. We will let her speak.

Good morning, to you Readers, and yes, I was next in line (*smile*). I was just delighted, for I am one of the Goddesses. **I AM the Goddess Athena**. Now I too was Greek and lived during those ancient times. My energy was one of *peace, joy,* and *love*. While Plato had his schools, we had what one would call our *Temples*. We met in Temples and we would teach the young Initiates, the women. There were no men in our Temples, for we were bringing forth the Goddess energies in the young girls. We had strict principles. The young girls must be pure, must be virgins, must be intelligent, and must be receptive to receiving their education in the highest sense. There were always girls who were available, but we sought a special energy that they held. Women needed to be in touch with the Goddess part of them.

I know in your mythology there were all of these Goddesses who had talents and gifts that were beyond most of humanity. That is what mythology says of the Goddesses. However, in our Temples we were very real. Actually, your Essenes taught many of the things that we had taught. One of the major teachings was that we knew we were part of the feminine energy of God. We were part of that feminine principle, the Mother part of God. We knew that. For a while, this Goddess energy was prevalent on the planet, more so than the male energy. It was energy of knowing, intuition, caring, love, gentleness, but, oh, we were also very strong. There is a fallacy that if a woman is gentle, quiet, caring, and can absorb knowledge, in some way she is not as strong mentally or in energy as a male. That simply is not true. Strong women can be very gentle. They also can be feisty. They can use anger, but they use it correctly. They do not displace their anger on others. They merely use it for a particular dynamic, to make the energy shift. Anger, if it is used constructively, is a very effective tool in leading that person forward. Therefore, with our

The Ultimate Experience
THE GODDESS ATHENA

Initiates, we were precise; we were gentle; we were joyful; we were humorous; we were strong; and we could be angry.

The Initiates, these strong women, also had strong egos and strong wills. It was a difficult concept to get across to the Initiates that they need not come from ego. If they were meek, gentle, simplistic, and child-like, they need not rule people with an iron fist, all ego-led. They can be perceptive. Many men are afraid of strong women, for it is a male concept that he must dominate the female.

It goes somewhat back to the Stone Age, the cave men that had cunning, but not necessarily intelligence or awareness. They used their brutal strength to survive and to bring forth more children. The women who they brought to them usually were captives. Women were for men's pleasure. Many were their own daughters. They also were used by the man to propagate his clan. There was little Goddess energy during that time.

In ancient Greece, in some respects we dominated the males, for the males held us in awe. They put us on a pedestal. You were either a male god or a female Goddess. They raised us above themselves. That was just the thinking of the ignorant. Since we were close to the Mother God and since our intuition was well defined, we were also great *seers*. We could foretell the future. Therefore, the general populace thought of us as *soothsayers* telling their futures. We did much more than that, for we held the energy for certain areas such as the Temples. The Goddess Temples held the energy from Mother God. Therefore, when people entered the Temple, they entered in a hushed way, a devotional way, a respective way, and a frightened way, for they simply could not understand the feeling that would come over them as they entered the Temple. They were always rather glad to leave again.

The males rarely came to the Temple. They would send their wives or other females of their family to go to the Temple. *Go to the Temple and ask Athena what I should do.* They always wanted someone to tell them what to do, for life was difficult for

115

many. Again, you had the wealthy and those in poverty. Those in poverty always needed help in how to take another step to better themselves. The wealthy ones always seemed to need help with the various assignations in which they found themselves. Sexual affairs and the sexual intrigues ran rampant among the wealthy.

Therefore, you see that it was not so out of place to have a Temple that could be kept pure and the energies high, for the people were just not that in tune to produce this tranquility in their own environments. Many mothers of young girls held out the hope to their daughters: *if you would do such and such, if you are kind, if you are chaste, and you give thanks to the Goddess, maybe you will be chosen to be an Initiate of the Temple.* It was considered an honor, a great honor.

Now what does all of that—those ancient times, those ancient beliefs, that ancient energy—have to do with this present-time book on Realities (*smile*)? It merely is pointing out another reality that is no longer true. There were people during that time where the Temple simply was not a reality for them, nor did they ever visit it. The philosophy was not a reality for them, nor did they ever attempt to learn it. The blessed female energy was not a reality for them, for they did not have the awareness or the training to know or to recognize the gifts that the Mother was giving them. However, the training had an aura of specialness about it. It was as though it were veiled from the common eyes. It was considered a sanctuary from what people would call the *real world*. What **was** real? For the Initiates in Athena's Temple, **that** was the real world, their real world. For the public, that was not in their reality and therefore not a real world to them.

As the world lost its touch with the Goddess energy, the male energy became dominant. It was a patriarch, a male domination. The Goddess energy receded. Souls that were born into later centuries no longer carried the Goddess energy, for they were being born into a male's world—the patriarchs' world. For those of you who are reading these books or have heard it before, in order for there to be Heaven on Earth, there needs to be a balance between male and female energies. Each person that is born carries both. You know that. You have been told that and you have read that. However, in each person, one of the energy principles takes over and becomes more dominant, no matter what gender your body is. However, people need to become more aware of this fact and strive to bring a balance in the body. If you are a female, use your male energy in a balance. If you are a male, use your female energy in a balance. Create a body that is balanced in your life. You can do this. This is not some nebulous Utopist idea. It is God's way of bringing balance to the Earth.

As far as reality is concerned, did those realities of the Goddess Temples really exist? I can say that YES, they did. Do they exist today? No, they do not. Do they exist in the fifth dimension? They exist in a way that perhaps you would not recognize, for in the fifth dimension, the Goddess energy is manifest, but it is blended with the male energy. Thereby, both are used. In the higher dimensions, since I was long time dead in your eyes, but long time alive in the higher dimensions in my eyes, I consider myself still a Goddess—the Goddess energies—for that is my purpose. That has always been my purpose to bring the female awareness to the body, to bring the female balance to the body. That is my purpose. Therefore, in the fifth dimension, yes, I still do exist, as does Yeshua. However, is he crucified there? No, he is not. Is my Temple still there? No, it is not, but the **energy** is still there. Ah, so now I have introduced another concept. Do you think that the **energy** for the crucifixion that might have happened in the third dimension that was perceived by some is still viable for the fifth dimension? No, it is not.

Let us bring that concept to present time. There are skirmishes that are war building in the Middle East today *(7-14-06)*. Do you think that there is any Goddess energy there in present time? Not in that mentality, for that mentality is still in the third dimension. What you are seeing is third dimension drama. Instead of crucifying people, they take them and behead them. Is that not crucifixion mentality? Would that be happening in the fifth dimension? No, it would not. As you continue on the continuum, that will not come forward. Therefore, Readers, there is always that conflict going on. As one dimension gets ready to be birthed into another dimension, the energies must be transmuted. They must be brought to another level with Light. They only can be transmuted with Light. **They only can be transmuted if they have manifested.** What you are seeing is the manifestation of the dark energies. I believe it is Yeshua who said, *it is the last dying gasps of the dark Cabal (channeled during a group presentation 6-07-06).* How does the dark fight? It fights with killing and destruction, for you see that brings fear. If they can make enough people afraid, they have won. All of the people who are cowering in their bomb shelters or in their basements in those countries to escape the different rockets and missiles are in fear.

Many of those people are innocent in this lifetime. However, keep in mind that they did sign on for this play in their pre-birth agreement. That is always a difficult concept for people to accept. *Do you mean I signed up for this? It does not seem possible!* You see, dear Readers, there is no Goddess energy in that whole conflagration, is there? None. It is third dimensional, dark Cabal brutality rising in order to be transmuted by Light, Love, and prayers of the faithful—who are praying correctly. Keep in mind many of those dark ones are also praying. They are praying to win.

People in America need to keep that whole area in their prayers and pray for God's Light and Love to bring peace to where there is war, Love to where there is hate. Some day, some year, some century the Goddess energy will come forth again. It may never be prevalent, for there needs to be a balance. However, she needs to be recognized, also. When you recognize the Goddess in women, you are recognizing the Mother God. She is just as much a part of you as God the Father is.

All right, my dear Readers, it has been my honor to come forth and give you a little bit of my energy for this book.

The Ultimate Experience
THE GODDESS ATHENA

I am known as **Goddess Athena** and I thank you. *(Thank you Lady, thank you.)*

(OK, Yeshua is that what you wanted?) *That is exactly what we wanted. She brought it into present-time, which was perfect. That is all for today, my dear one. See you tomorrow (smile).* (Thank you, Lord, adieu.) *Adieu to you too.*

(Note: Goddess Athena's Temple is the Parthenon in Athens, Greece. While she is portrayed in history as being war-like, wearing the winged helmet, she was more of a mediator and a defender of the cities. The Trojan horse was her inspiration. Much information may be found on the various Internet websites.)

The Ultimate Experience

MARIAM'S REMARKS

Good morning once again, my dear soul, I am here with another surprise for you and our Readers for this book, which is turning out to be quite wonderful—more than our expectations. Actually, we do not have expectations; we just know (smile). How could the book not be wonderful with all of those Beings coming forth? You have been hearing them clearly and purely. Occasionally, there is a little mental dance in order to find the appropriate word, but that certainly is normal with all channels. You are doing a magnificent job, dear one, and we thank you.

Now we are going to backtrack a little, for I wish to bring Mariam back. She has more she wishes to say. Therefore, without further words from me, I will step back and let Mariam speak.

Good morning once again to all of our dear Readers, **I AM Mariam,** the adopted cousin-sister of Yeshua and an aspect of this channel. As we watched and heard the various Presenters, I was reminded of my own experiences with the Essenes. We were indeed taught the Goddess energies, for we were in a higher awareness state than people outside of our group at Mount Carmel. It was important for us, you see, as Initiates to have this information, for we knew we would be part of the experience, especially with Mother Mary when she brought forth Yeshua. While she was older than I, she was not that much older, maybe by only fifteen years or so, and we both married when we were quite young.

While I was an Essene, I was not what one would call a *dreamer.* I was quite matter-of-fact and as the saying goes, *I had a mind of my own.* I could tell the difference between a Truth and a lie when people were speaking to me—usually outside of the Essene establishment, for those of us at Mount Carmel strove to speak only Truth. Of course, if we did not have the correct information and spoke, it could come out as not being Truth.

However, it was not a deliberate lie on our part, for we were taught Truth.

Much of the teaching was from my grandmother, Anna, who had a loving heart but expected one to abide by her strict discipline. She carried the Goddess energy. If she were in mythology during those times, she would be a Goddess in her own right. She taught us much; she taught us well. She taught us to walk in the ways of the Goddess. Now keep in mind just as the Goddess Athena told you, being a Goddess was not being some mythological aberration. It was merely a term for the energy that she carried and was helping us to bring forth. The energy of course is from the Mother God, or one could say the other half of God, for He is the Father-Mother God. Some use the term Mother-Father God. We in our own right, carry that male and female energy, as we have said, for we are replicas of Father-Mother God.

The life at Mount Carmel emphasized bringing balance into our bodies. One energy principle need not be dominated by the other. In other words, if you were a female, you were expected to use your male energy in helping you to go forward in whatever endeavor you were attempting. That male energy along with the female's intuition and artistic bent enabled you to make the creation happen—always with balance. Men were taught to use their feminine intuition, not the feminine wiles, but the caring, loving, intuitive, creative side—what today you would call your *right brain*. Your right brain is your feminine side and your left-brain is your masculine side, the intellect.

It is human nature to want to immediately assume that *if your left brain is the masculine side of you, that means that males are more intelligent.* No, that is not what it means. Sometimes your intellect becomes so dominant that it does not allow your intelligence to shine forth. In esoteric terms, the intellect needs to be transmuted into pure intelligence. It will shine in your auric field as a pale yellow. Readers who read people and see energies can see that energy. If it is dark and a deep yellow, they are looking at the intellect, which is not as positive, versus the pale yellow color of the intelligence band.

However, as an Essene, whether one was male or female, the teaching was to always bring both parts of yourself into balance. You realize that since we started there at such a young age, we were not very mature. A maturity of the body needed to take place. If you start bringing awareness to young people or young bodies, it becomes a way of life with them, for the balances are started very early. In your modern-day times, the children are not balanced. They start school in an unbalanced way. Of course, much of this stems from their parents, for you are talking about human nature, personalities, and egos—whether the father figure is dominant over the mother or the female is dominant over the meek male—all of this comes into play and influences the child. Consequently, the child comes to school with an imbalance already between his or her masculine or feminine energies.

I am not going to go into the whole homosexual dynamic, for so much comes into play with that—what are your pre-birth agreements? Is this a soul experience that your soul is desiring; is this a hormone imbalance; or does the soul wish to bring out the creative side of itself that it was not able to do in a previous lifetime? There is so much involved here. Do not judge your homosexual friends, my dear ones. They know they have taken on a difficult life, but they have set this up. They have chosen this play for the various reasons I have just named. You are not to judge those reasons.

However, one can see as a small child sometimes how a small boy is developing his feminine side and it is not in balance. He wants to play with his sister's dolls. They fascinate him. He is playing with them not to be homosexual, he is playing with them because he knows that's a girl and that's a boy, and he plays in his own mind with these toy-children. When a parent becomes frightened and thinks that the child is gravitating toward a homosexual bent in life, many times the parent puts too much emphasis on this which creates an imbalance in itself, or it makes the child feel as if he or she is wrong in some way—that this is a secret that one must not tell. It is blown out of proportion.

In our world, the world of higher dimensions, homosexuality is looked upon in different ways, for we all carry the energies. There can be souls that embrace, and it makes no difference as to whether they are wearing jeans or wearing a robe. There is nothing considered unacceptable or wrong about any of this. The Goddess Athena was saying that she still carries her Goddess energy and considers herself a Goddess. That does not mean that she does not have a balance with her masculine principle. She does. However, when you meet her, she presents herself as a woman. I, myself, Mariam, am an aspect that is still feminine. I am a female. However, I have been a male in other lifetimes. Mariam then came in as a male in order to experience that energy for various reasons. It is what souls do. It is called *learning experiences* and their different purposes have them experiencing different life genders. What is it like to be a woman and to bear a child? What is it like to be a man and carry the seeds for children, the responsibility of creating another life? These are all different experiences that souls desire. Therefore, when we were at Mount Carmel being taught the different energies, we learned at a very young age the importance of balance. I have often thought that one of the cruelest concepts that humanity has is that people must be the way you think they ought to be. It is so cruel.

You see this quite often in your schools. If you are not out playing football or baseball but choose to study music and be in the band, you are considered less than the jocks who are out strutting and flexing their muscles. It is cruel, and it creates an imbalance. For the girls who feel they must be cheerleaders or queens or in the queen's court for different festivities, how does the other girl feel the one whose purpose is not to be looked upon as a sex idol—what about that girl? It can become so cruel. This is where we think your schools need to be recreated, for the children forsake their morals. You see pictures on television news of young boys punching other defenseless boys on a bus, simply because the attackers are bigger and stronger than the ones they punch.

The inequality, the imbalance is so prevalent. Many times I would weep with frustration when I was walking among the Disciples. All were men who had, we will say, *issues* with their egos. They did not take kindly to a woman's teaching. They played out their games of bravado, silly jokes, and noisiness and, in some cases, contempt. There were wives who followed the Disciples. However, many of the wives stayed home with their families.

With the Lord Yeshua, he kept teaching by example. *You go to the women and treat them as equals. If they are arguing, you must go to them, listen to each one, and then tell a parable. In that way, the energy will change and the people will become less angry.* Keep in mind, everyone who was in Yeshua's *entourage*, although he would not call it that—his followers, his Wayshowers—were struggling with their own balance. *How do I bring balance to this?* They did not use those terms, for they did not know about the Mother-Father energies. They had Yeshua on a pedestal, for they recognized a great Teacher in him.

During the times of strife, when Yeshua was realizing it was no longer safe to be in an area and he would have to leave, he would tell the Disciples to let go of these thoughts, this judgment that they had against their fellow men or women. In modern times, people who read the Bible and read about the Disciples, the Apostles, are apt to think of them as being perfect. They were **not** perfect. They were as imperfect as I was. They were learning as I was. They were attempting to balance out their lives as I was. There was camaraderie among the men and the women and they gravitated toward each other.

Mary Magdalene was the confidant for me. When Mother Mary was present, just her energy field would bring calmness to the group. How much that is needed today. There have been instances in your world where people see visions of Mother Mary and Yeshua. No one has ever seen me. I have not shown myself, for people would not know me anyway (*smile*). What would be the purpose? It would only scare them, most likely (*laughingly*). However, with Mother Mary so much is associated with her. Just her presence will bring miracles and feelings of peace.

Now let us tie all of this altogether. I have been speaking of the balances that people must bring into their bodies, so that they may bring balance into their lives. I am speaking of the energies of Mother-Father God—the feminine and masculine energies that we all carry as well as the Goddess energies. These must come into balance. If there were a balance of those energies today, you would not see the wars that are happening in the Middle East area. However, as you have been told, that is still third-dimension mentality. That dark energy must surface so that those of Light can transmute it.

Therefore, dear Readers, I hope this chapter has made you think and look at your own balance of energies in your body. Are you using your female and male energies in balance, or are they out of whack? We touched upon homosexuality. Can you let your belief systems change if you have been judgmental? Homosexuals are **not** sinning, as written in the Bible. Their soul has asked for this experience, and they are living their soul's purpose. It is time that humanity raises its consciousness and becomes more aware of pre-birth agreements, of the desires of the soul to experience, no matter what you may think. If the soul is connected to its Higher Self in awareness, it is serving its purpose.

With that, dear Readers, I will step aside once again and let Yeshua come forth if he wishes to add anything to this. Until we meet again in these pages, **I AM Mariam.**

(*Thank you, Mariam, and now Yeshua, do you have anything more you wish to add?*) *I wish to add that the judgments that humanity lays on each other are more damaging than they realize. What you judge circles around and comes back as Cause and Effect. What you judge, you will become, if not in this lifetime,*

then another. Now, that ought to be a scary thought for everyone!
What you judge, you will become!

*There is a difference between judging and discernment, for in judging you are making a declaration that that person is wrong, or sinful, or immoral in some way. With discernment, you observe, you name it and you let it go. You do **not** call it wrong, or call anything wrong. You discern that there is a skirmish or wars in the Middle East. **Remember, the dark must manifest in order to be transmuted.***

(The tape ran out and Yeshua told me to end this chapter.)

The Ultimate Experience

BROTHER JAMES

*Dearest one and dearest Readers, we come once again with another Presenter and another surprise. As I told you yesterday, they are lined up! I do wish to say a few words about how our book is progressing. In the beginning, we thought we would have a book just about Mariam, my sister. However, as you see, the book has a mind of its own (smile). We thought it more correct, in respect to timing, to speak about dimensions. Therefore, **we spoke of the crucifixion, as to whether it happened or not. We say that it did not,** but there are those authors who received different information and have written beautiful books on the aftermath of the crucifixion. At this point, we will say to use your own discernment according to your level of awareness.*

*Whenever anyone chooses to change his or her belief system, and most people change just one of their beliefs at a time, it is usually not a snap decision. It is something that grows on them; or we could say that awareness begins to enlighten them, and they start to question previous knowledge. Knowledge does not become wisdom until you use it. It then becomes a Truth for you. On the other hand, when it no longer is true for you, then it has become a lie, has it not? What we are saying is that when your beliefs have turned into a lie—and some people are put off by such a strong word; they like to make it more gentle by calling it an **untruth**—when you have reached those situations in your beliefs, you then let them go, for you have transmuted them. You now have a new belief around the same dynamic. In this case, it is the crucifixion. As more and more knowledge is given to you, you then can let go of the old concepts that are wrong. Let the new knowledge settle in as wisdom.*

__I have said repeatedly in this book that the crucifixion did not happen in any real sense.__ Recently, a question was raised to the author, "What about the Stigmata that many people and priests experience—where a person's hands bleed at the point

127

The Ultimate Experience
BROTHER JAMES

*where the nails supposedly pierced Jesus' hands?" That is a phenomenon where a belief system is so strong that it becomes mind over matter. It is so strong that the belief can manifest physically. Now I am sure there are people who have stigmata, and they are not going to give that up very quickly, for it has brought them notoriety. When you are a priest in a certain order, is it not wonderful to have the blood come out your palms? It shows off your devotion for your other brother to see—at least **you** think it shows your devotion.*

Some doctors could call it hysteria. We call it using your mind as the master instead of your heart. I have said in Glenda Green's wonderful book, Love Without End, *that your mind must never be the master of your Being. Your heart rules, always. Therefore, when people have stigmata going on, it is their mind and their ego in control. In some unconscious way it is giving them what psychologists call "negative strokes." Unconsciously, it makes them feel important. It makes them feel that they have a certain connection with me that others do not have. Egos again, **for if I did not** bleed **then, how could they bleed now?***

*I certainly did not bleed in the palms, but I did bleed across my back, across my face and across my legs when I was whipped in order to impress upon me to "get out of Dodge, Jesus, before we kill you." That was a very strong message because I felt their energy. I felt their hatred. I felt their zealousness. I felt their negative righteousness. (*Yeshua's energy becomes forceful and the words by thought are staccato.*) The men who actually did the whipping were usually cruel men to begin with and had a sadistic type of personality. They enjoyed the whipping. If a man was called forth to perform the flailing and did not do a very good job, he would be punished. In order to save his own skin, many times he put all of his strength behind the whip.*

There is so much involved around that concept of the crucifixion—even the stigmata. On some of the Christian television programs, the Evangelist makes the argument that one on the cross is not nailed through the palms but through

128

the wrists, for that will support the body better. Now that was true for the criminals who were being crucified. However, the Evangelists and even historians have talked themselves into a particular theory and have applied it to me. I too only can say **thank God, I listened!** *Thank God that I had the awareness to know when to leave.*

I think that is all that I will say for now. I **do like** *the way we have set these chapters up. I* **do like** *the way we can come in and say our piece before bringing in a Presenter or make our comments afterwards. We are all enjoying this so much, Readers. I hope you are too.*

Now what do we have in store for you today? I think it is time to bring another great Being forward, for he patiently has been standing in line waiting his turn (smile). Without further adieu, I will let him present himself. **I AM Yeshua.**

Readers, dear Readers, I now have made it to the front of the line (*smile*). You cannot know what an honor it is to come forth and to give you some of our wisdom. I am another one of Yeshua's Disciples, his Apostle, and his half-brother. **I AM James**, the one who was martyred by the zealots, for they did not understand the teachings that we were giving forth. I grew up with Yeshua. He was a dear brother to me in every way. Yet, as young boys do, we joked with each other; we punched each other; we argued with each other. We would try to best the other in whatever we were doing. I was sturdier than Yeshua. Yeshua was growing so fast that he was always eating. He was always hungry and then I ate right along with him (*laughing*). Our mother always saw to it that there was food that we could eat. Keep in mind that we did not have refrigeration, so our food was more of the natural type of food. There was always bread in the breadbaskets, which we hung from the ceiling so that the snakes could not crawl into them. There was dried fruit or fresh fruits if they were in season.

Is it not interesting how in each generation, it is what it is? If you are born into that generation, you do not know any difference. If you in modern times were teleported back to those ancient days, you would find that you would have a hard time adjusting, for humanity has become what we would call rather *soft* in its ways. You like your comforts—your air-conditioning, your refrigeration, your freezers, your furnaces, your huge supermarkets, your air-conditioned cars, your heated cars. In winter, you even have cars where you push a button and your seats are heated for you! It is quite amazing, for in our time, we were either walking in the snow, or we were sitting on a cold donkey bundled the best we could be. However, we knew no different. That was a way of life. I do think we were a heartier lot than many of you are today.

Our childhood was quite normal, actually. We prayed. We followed the Laws for the Sabbath. It was not until Yeshua was older that he started changing some of the interpretations of the Law (*much laughter*). He used to amaze me to see how he would argue with the priests. One would think *how do you have the guts to do that?* Of course, we brothers would be incredulous. *How do you do that?* He was Yeshua! (*Laughingly*) He knew what the interpretation ought to be. He knew God's flexibility and he loved Him with all of his heart.

He never disobeyed God. When God told him to do something—he received it either in his dreams or in meditations—he would do it. He was known in our family for communing with God—more so than the other members of our family. One could often see him walking among the trees. Many a time I could hear him from a distance. I could not make out what he was saying, but I could see his lips moving, for he was talking aloud. Often if he did not know anyone was around, he would talk aloud in the house. (It reminds me of what this channel does. She is always talking aloud; anything she thinks, she says it aloud, *laughter*, for she lives alone. *There are advantages to living alone,* she is telling me. *One of them is that I can talk aloud; another is I can eat when I want to, and another is I do not have to cook anymore for anyone else but myself. Those are advantages at times,* said with a smile).

Back in our time, life had its ups and downs just like it does in anyone's lifetime. There is ebb, a flow, ebb, and a flow. Just when you think everything is going along just fine, then *wham,* there comes the surprise-blow. Our surprise blow was when Yeshua was becoming too much of a disturbing element for the Sanhedrin. You know, Readers, after I had finished that lifetime, I did come back and had other lifetimes. However, I was adamant that I did not want to come back in any way to be in what we would say is the *religious way.* I wanted to be entirely away from the strict control that the Rabbis put on you. I did not want to come back as a Jew and be in that religion again. However, seeing the way that Christianity took a negative turn from the priests, I did not want to come back in that setting either!

I chose a different setting. I chose a setting where I could be free. I wanted to be a dreamer. I wanted to invent things. I wanted to create. Therefore, I came back after several hundreds of years. I said, *OK, I'll come back again, but I don't want to be martyred! I don't want to die that way again.* Now the life I chose had to have some of the Cause and Effect from the previous lifetime, of course, for that is what a life experience is all about.

You know the Christians have all the Disciples and Apostles— however you wish to name them—up in Heaven, right next to God, each in his own mansion in Heaven. I suppose for a while we created those, just like any soul would when he has left a lifetime. You create something better than you had before. However, what the theologians do not tell you, for they do not know themselves or believe it, is when you have had a well-known life, it does not mean you stop there. It means you come back again and try another aspect of learning.

One could say that I did the Christian thing and now I wanted something else. When I say the *Christian thing,* I mean following Jesus and the start of Christianity's Teachings after he left. However, now I wanted something else. Therefore, I did come back. I am not going to say what my name was. It is not important. It is only important to the soul's Book that it keeps—your life's records. After you have died and if you wish to check out those Akashic records, they are there for all to see, for you just scroll down and read them.

It is an interesting phenomenon that when someone dies and you go to Nirvana, you are in the same energy band of consciousness that you were in when you died. Therefore, if you were in a lower band, you go to the lower level. If you were higher, you go to the higher levels. We were able to go to the higher levels because of the awareness the Lord had taught us. I still think of him as my brother, for now in the higher realms we are all brothers and sisters of God.

Many times, souls forget their previous lifetime after a while. However, a lifetime such as mine is not forgotten because the people, humanity, keep bringing it forward. They talk about the Disciples. They study the sayings of the Apostles and their lives. Therefore, it keeps us in the foreground. In that way, I do remember that lifetime. I remember our dear Mother, who you call *Mother Mary,* who had a great deal of inner awareness and love that she spread evenly among her children. I remember my dear Father, Joseph, and his carpentry shop—how it smelled from different woods.

Therefore, you see, Readers, someday you may be standing in line in order to say a few words in a book that that particular author is writing. There will be a different set of issues, for as *time marches on*, as the saying goes, so do the historical events. We must admit that with all of the Earth changes that are going to be happening and with the dark Cabal with its last gasping breath, it will be interesting. We are watching very closely. For some of the dynamics that are in play right now in your modern times, we do not see the probability—only the possibility of how it will end. You have heard this so many times. **Free will causes the probability.**

The Ultimate Experience
BROTHER JAMES

We have been talking about my childhood with Yeshua, my dear brother. We spoke a little of the crucifixion and what happened. There was such a void when he left. Yeshua spoke of the stigmata. Now it is up to you, Readers, to transmute your belief systems. Ask yourself, *in what dimension am I?* If you are in fear and believe everything that you hear, read, and see on television, you are in the third dimension. If you believe that everything in the Bible is true, you are in the third dimension. If you have a feeling of loyalty to your President Bush and his government, you pretty well can say that you are in the third dimension. All of that needs to be transmuted in order for you to go into the fourth dimension. That is where the world is going. You need to change your thinking. If you ponder this and ask yourself *in what dimension am I evolving,* then listen, you will know; you will get an answer. Maybe that will help spark you to move forward.

With that dear, Readers, I have nothing more to add. I thank you. I am honored by the privilege of speaking with you and being a part of this book.

I am the Apostle James, the half-brother of Yeshua. *Let us name this chapter,* **Brother James**. *I will step back now and see if Yeshua wishes to say anything more. (*Thank you, Lord*) You are welcome dear channel; you are welcome. And I knew you well when you were Mariam.*

Well, so my brother speaks. Did he tell tales out of school? (Laughingly) He was a wonderful brother with a great sense of humor, which I think came through as he was speaking with all of you. All right, beloveds, this is it for another chapter. Until tomorrow, **I AM Yeshua**.

*Good morning, my dear one, you have a little postscript that you would like to add to this last chapter. (*Yes, please Lord, for I was looking up the Apostle James on the Internet. There are so many James that I became confused.*) First, all the different James, as in James the Just and James the Lesser, are just the*

The Ultimate Experience
BROTHER JAMES

*historians' way of trying to separate them. I would say that Brother James is definitely the Just one, for he did minister and counsel there in Jerusalem after I left. He is not written as the Apostle, but he **was an Apostle**, my brother. I know that it is also written that the brothers were not considered Apostles simply because they did not believe what I was saying until many years later. That simply is not true. James was my brother, but one could say he was my **stepbrother**, for indeed he was Joseph's son by a former marriage in which he became a widower. **He is my brother. He is James the Just, the Apostle**. He is not the son of Zebedee. **James was martyred**. He was stoned to death, by the order of the high priest, Ananus of the Pharisees. He was not the James that was killed by a sword.*

(One more thing, please, Yeshua. Your brother, James, was being very modest and did not say what his next lifetimes were. I am not sure if he ended up being an inventor, or did he become King James and formulate the Bible, the King James Version?) *He indeed came back as King James. He is known as that. In fact, he is channeled many times as King James, still the Apostle, my brother. He was the King James who put all the books together in a readable form and made the King James Version of the Bible. In that way, he did create. That was his creation.*

SAINT LUKE, THE PHYSICIAN

Well, it looks as if I am going down my list of Apostles here. Who is next in line? We have had John the Beloved. We have had my brother James. Do you think it might be time to bring in one of the other ones? How about Luke—how would you like to hear from Saint Luke, another great Being and the writer of many of the books in the Bible? Keep in mind, though, that his words are distorted and many of the passage are not accurate. One of his most famous past lives in your modern days was as Edgar Cayce. How do you think Edgar Cayce knew all of those medical prescriptions that he gave forth? He was a physician. He was Saint Luke, the Physician. Therefore, without further words from me, I will bring him forth and see what he wishes to say.

Readers, this is such a privilege and such fun for me. **I AM Luke**, one of the Master's devoted servants and followers. I loved him so. My love for him has not lessened, for now I am able to be with him whenever I wish and to speak with him whenever I wish. Those were such strife-filled days. There was so much fear. I liken it perhaps to your modern times with the fears and the wars that are going on in your Middle East right now. There are always those who must control others and who think their way is the only way. I was not that influential as a young man. I grew into that role. I did study medicine—what your modern doctors would call *antiquated medicine (smile)*.

We had some home remedies that worked quite well, actually. Do you realize that your present-day doctors are using those little bugs, those creatures that eat dead flesh? You call them *maggots*. Well, we used maggots also. They tickled, but they would clean away the dead flesh. Then they would get so full that they would just roll off. We were very protective of them. I kept them in a cup with holes in it. They could not go through the holes, but air could come in. I did feed them well (*smile*), for I had many patients that avoided amputation because they were willing to try anything, even maggots.

We also used leeches, but I did not leech my patients as severely as some of the physicians did in the early parts of your, say, twelfth century on up. They would actually bleed a patient to death in order to save him! I did not do that.

I made poultices with some herbs. We used dirt, just dirt mixed with a little bit of wine. The wine, you see, had the alcohol in it. We also used honey. Therefore, all of these ancient practices have come full circle. They now are being used in your holistic medicines. Many of the home remedies were used also by the pioneer women. The doctors did the best as they could. Of course, just like it is today, if they had a healing touch, they were better doctors than their colleagues were.

After the Holy Spirit came upon me, I found that my healings of my patients increased. I was able to diagnose better. I did not realize that my energy field also healed the patients. Now keep in mind when I say I was healing patients, it is always God who does the healing. I am merely His servant. God does the healing. I am speaking of God, the Father. I know many Christians think of their Jesus as God. In an esoteric way, in the way that we are all part of God, you could use that term. However, in the Hebrew sense, there is only one God—God the Father. Jesus and some of the Disciples, that Holy Family, were still just a human family. They were not Gods, not even Messiahs. Oh, how the Jews wanted a Messiah. Many of the people who surrounded Jesus (and I am calling him *Jesus* here, for that is how he was known in your Bibles, not *Yeshua),* came to him because they believed so desperately that he would save them—liberate them from the Romans. That was not his role. He kept telling them that he was not the Messiah. People hear what they want to hear. It is a *selective* type of hearing, is it not? They hear what they wish to hear.

My life was not that complicated after Yeshua left the country, and I do not mean that he left by dying on the cross, for we know

The Ultimate Experience
SAINT LUKE, THE PHYSICIAN

that he did not. (The purpose of this book is to let you Readers know that not only did he **not die** on the cross, but also **he did not go to the cross**.) When we say that he left, he left our lives. We felt such a void as he left the country to seek another calling to wherever God was leading him. Therefore, we wrote our epistles. We tried to recall his words but to use your term we were *paraphrasing* what he had said. Many times, we got it correct and other times we did not. When the scribes came along and tried to interpret **our** meanings, they would get it correct sometimes, and other times **they** would not.

The Bible, actually, is a hodgepodge—a hodgepodge (*smile*). People think the words are verbatim. However, they are people's projections, people's selective listening, people's judgments and opinions. They thought it was all written as Truth. If you bring some humor into this, it can be quite amusing to think about it. However, the Christians are so serious when it comes to their "God." We who knew him were serious too at times, but we loved him as a human being. He was an extraordinary Soul in a human body and had the delights of a wonderful marriage. History will not even allow him to have that. It is sad at the same time that it is rather humorous. Church fathers put him on such a high pedestal they would never let him step off—to have children, oh my, would that ever be a sin! It is so amazing. However, since we are talking about dimensions in this book, we can say, *that's a good example of third-dimensional thinking!*

Higher Beings such as the Master all have job descriptions. (He has many titles, but I refer to him as the Master; I also call him Lord; I call him Teacher.) They come to Earth with job descriptions, with purposes. God sends them. They are not God per se. One could use the lower-case *g* versus the capital *G,* but we are all gods. New Agers realize this. However, those in the third dimension think of it as being blasphemous. Therefore, we say that these gods in their own right came to Earth. They have their priorities. They know their purposes. With humanity's free will, many times souls must jiggle this and dance around that in

137

order to bring their purpose into fruition. Yeshua was no different in that respect. He had to do a great deal of juggling.

One of his biggest hurdles of course was the older Rabbis—the priests, the Sanhedrin, the Pharisees—all thinking they knew more than he did. This is where their free will would take over. They played their roles, but sometimes more zealously than they were intended. It is a human weakness that when someone is desperately trying to control others, thinking that his way is the only right way, he is unapproachable in order to reason with him. I have heard this channel say that *one cannot be reasonable with one who is not reasonable.* It is human nature.

After my Luke experience, I had other lifetimes, with the Edgar Cayce* life being the more known to you, perhaps. However, I came back before that. I was always interested in the medical field. I wanted to know more about what made a person tick—not necessarily to heal someone from a disease or illness, but I wanted to know about how a person thinks, what we have come to know as the *ego*, the *psyche*, and all of Freud's magnificent work. I wanted to know all of that. Therefore, I had a lifetime learning those different theories. I was not well known. Readers may find it hard to believe, but we do not always seek fame and fortune. Many times one learns that going to a deeper level requires more wisdom, and you do not need the trappings of the rich and famous to facilitate this. I did not want to be famous. I just wanted to study what you would term *psychology.* You cannot learn all of that in Nirvana, for you must learn it during the times that you are a human being. The human Being has the different complex thought processes—the *ego* being the most well known part of us. It was fascinating to me. When I came into the Edgar Cayce body, I could help people psychologically, for many times their problems stemmed from past lives. I could tell them from where that stemmed.

People from back in antiquity were always afraid of demons, bad spirits, and being overtaken by unseen powers. You see their consciousness was not all that developed. They would get in trouble when they sought to experiment and delve into witchcraft. They were more fascinated in how they could see into people in order to control them. There were all manner of amulets you could hang around your neck, or little pouches—tiny purses in which you could put little pieces of bone or such. **And** they worked because you had dark forces that occupied your space and were fulfilling your intentions. It was a dangerous game.

Therefore, when you read in your Bible where Jesus cast out the spirits here and there, he did not see it in that way. However, he knew when someone was delving into the darker games of life, the darker occult. That is why the Bible warns so heavily against it. Then like with everything else, people lump it all together and cannot have any of it. Your great *seers* and *oracles*, as Goddess Athena was telling you, served a purpose for people. Those *oracles* were from a higher evolution—higher Light. They guided you. Further more, what they said came true. They did not harm you, but they could warn you. However, the witches of antiquity would harm you if you did not do as they said. They would put curses on you. It was a very common practice in antiquity to have a curse put on you. What they did not realize was when they put that curse on someone else, then in either that lifetime or another, they would experience their own curse! Therefore, it was not too pleasant an aftermath to curse someone, for it became a double curse. The giver became the receiver of it.

I have traveled through the centuries, coming in every once in a while in order to see what humanity was up to. You learn so much more when you are having the actual experience. I did not tarry too long in a body. I came in just long enough to learn what I wanted to learn about a particular disease or illness. When they were having the dreadful plague, the Black Plague that swept throughout Europe, I came in to experience that. I died of that. I wanted that information; I wanted that wisdom. You would not believe how quickly it happened. What is that saying *here today and gone tomorrow?* That is what that plague did. People were petrified, for they did not know how to handle it.

The Ultimate Experience
SAINT LUKE, THE PHYSICIAN

They did not know it was carried by the fleas on the rats and mice that proliferated throughout the streets, especially in the poorer sections and obviously in the markets. People always had fleas in those days. Many times in your wealthier families, the cook would go to the market to buy the next day's meals. She would be bitten by a flea and be dead that night or the next day. The smart ones left the cities and went to the country and escaped the rats and mice that were busy gnawing the garbage in the populated cities, thus not spreading their fleas to their country cousins.

That was not a very pleasant experience for me, but one I chose. This may be a new concept for some of you Readers. You might be saying to yourself *do you mean to say I chose to die in the Bubonic Plague, the Black Death?* I say to you *yes, you did.* However, I did not die until I had observed what was happening. I had many cases of people from the poor to the wealthy, who were hysterical, for no one knew how to stop the plague. I could do little for them. The wealthy were able to leave the areas and the poor could not. The plague killed thousands and thousands of people.

In these modern times, how tragic it is when your government would in some way sanction having scientists create a disease like AIDS, SARS, and chemtrails—different ways of killing the public. The pharmaceutical companies are growing wealthy on the illnesses of AIDS and HIV, bringing in millions of dollars. The patients are spending thousands of dollars on their treatments just to keep them alive.

Yeshua told a group a few months ago that AIDS was created by man. Yeshua told people you *agreed to experience this. You signed on for this. You were a courageous warrior to come in and do battle with this.* In my day as Edgar Cayce in the thirties and forties, your government was busy in making bombs and chemical warfare, but not dreaded diseases. Did I as Edgar Cayce know that this was coming? No, for you see when you are being a *seer*, someone must ask a question that then triggers the response.

The Ultimate Experience
SAINT LUKE, THE PHYSICIAN

No one ever asked *Mr. Cayce what about AIDS,* for we had never heard of it.

Therefore, every one hundred years has their particular illness. There was tuberculosis, diphtheria, measles, and whooping cough. Those have pretty well been controlled by different vaccinations. Many people do not approve of vaccinations. They are afraid of them, yet many of the older generation had them when they were young and lived to be in their eighties and nineties. Now it is thought that many of the cases of autism stem from these particular inoculations. Again, what is the pre-birth agreement here? Was it *I wish to experience autism? One of the ways I could become autistic would be to receive an inoculation.*

Of course, there are other ways, as most of you know. However, that has more or less become the popular way of becoming Autistic now for souls entering a body. There is a great learning experience in being Autistic. Do you realize, Readers, that your health professionals have earned their title? If you are a Psychologist, were you not a Psychologist or a student of Psychology in another lifetime? Of course you were. If you are an Internist and know a great deal about the conditions of the body, did you not study that in another lifetime? Of course you did. Did those educators or schoolteachers of mentally-challenged children not experience that themselves in another lifetime? Of course they did. You see that is why souls take on these difficult lessons. In the next lifetime, they can be the *healers,* just as I chose to experience the Bubonic Plague and after a few more lifetimes, I then came in as Edgar Cayce.

Therefore, each past life has a purpose. Therapists and hypnotherapists take their clients mentally to the past. They help them delve into that past life to find *what their purpose was in that lifetime that is causing their complaints in the present life.* Then they come back to the present and process their session.

It has been said that people must not be too focused on their past lives, for so many times they wish to go back to that lifetime where they were a king or queen forgetting that in that lifetime they were also beheaded because they **were** a king or a queen like Marie Antoinette.

There are as many lessons in your death experience as there are in your life experience, for in death it can become a challenge as to whether you will die correctly or not. People think they can just pop out. Some can and some cannot. One must die correctly, having absorbed all of one's information from that lifetime, taking the information with one—no more controlling, no more possessing your family, letting it all go.

In one lifetime I worked many years in a laboratory. I was looking through telescopes and watching the way cells can develop and multiply. I was looking to see if I could find a cure for something. So many people were dying from diabetes. *If only I could find a way to regenerate the pancreas*, I thought. *What can I do to stimulate the pancreas?* I was never able to come up with the answer, but it is in Nirvana. The answers to all diseases, all types of illnesses are in the great books in Nirvana. (Some people may still wish to call it Heaven.)

For everything that happens to humankind, there is an antidote, a cure for it in the Books in Heaven. There are great Libraries. You just look them up—look up what you wish to know. However, that process is made simpler for you since you need only to ask. You do not have to push buttons or what have you. You just go to a section, what you might call a *monitor, and say I wish to see this or I wish to see that.* It is then brought to you. The angels bring these books to you and then return them to their designated area. These libraries are very well stocked. They bring you information and then put it back on the shelf for you. Everything is listed.

I wanted to know about *diabetes* so I read about it. It is said that when you have *diabetes* you ought not to have too much sugar, for it can be detrimental to your system as can too little sugar. The diabetic comas are from either too much or too little sugars. If the pancreas does not function, you must take insulin in order to regulate it. Someday there will be a cure. You do not cure it by pharmaceutical means. You cure it when you have healed the pancreas. You have rejuvenated it.

This will be done in the future with energy work, through Light modalities, sound, and color. There will be buildings that you go to just as there are in Nirvana. You go to a room, get diagnosed, lie on a comfortable bed, and the Lights, sounds, music, and colors soothe over you rejuvenating whatever organ you came to have repaired. Your pancreas will be rejuvenated. Bodies will be made younger. Cells will be transmuted. Your skin will be tightened. Your muscles will be firmed, as will your flesh. All of this stems from the rejuvenation of your cells. It will not take years and years of treatment, for it can happen in just a few hours of your time.

Therefore, my dear Readers, I do not know if all of this will happen in your lifetime. It depends on what age you are now. It will not be in this channel's lifetime or in her grandchildren's lifetime, but it will happen, it will happen. Your diseases will be part of the past. They will go into antiquity. You may not need to use the creatures of Nature—the maggots, the leaches, the microbes in dirt for penicillin. You might still be using bees' honey, for it does have medicinal purposes.

It has been a privilege, Readers, to spend some time with you. I did not give you a great deal of Biblical history. However, I hope that what I have brought forth will be of an interest to you, to make you think, and to bring you hope.

With that, I will close.

I AM Luke, the Physician.

(Yeshua, anything you wish to add*?) No, dear one, it is an unusual chapter and full of different ideas. Luke always enjoyed learning about things and, as he says, what made him tick. With that, we leave you now, Readers, until tomorrow.*

(Author questions Yeshua about Saint Luke: Not being that familiar with the Bible, I did not know that Luke was around you or with you, for he was more of the Disciple of Saint Paul. Your comments, please.*) Luke did know me. Yes, he got a great deal of information from my Mother, but he did know me. We had met during all of his travels. We had met. He may not have known who I was at the time, but we had met.* (Therefore, when Saint Luke says in the chapter, "we who knew him," he really did know you then.)

*(*He said that the Holy Spirit came upon him and that is when he got all of his gifts for healing.) *That is true. When the Holy Spirit comes upon you, you receive many gifts, the gifts of sight. That is going to happen to you, my dear one, so get ready for it.*

(Was he ever married?) No, he was not married.

*(*In the chapter, he does not mention Saint Paul, although the Bible states that he was a Disciple of Saint Paul. Why would that be?) *He thought you already knew that. He thought people already knew that, so he talked about other things. He definitely had a relationship with Saint Paul. At times, it is purported to be a sexual relationship, for they thought that Saint Paul was a homosexual. He was not, nor was Saint Luke, nor did they have a sexual relationship. People seem to think that if a man is with a man it will be sexual. Those two men were not brought together for that reason. Saint Luke was to be a friend and a support for Saint Paul while he was imprisoned for so many years. Saint Luke would be the outside person that Saint Paul could count upon to befriend him.*

(There are two stories on his death. One is saying he was crucified in Greece. The second theory is that he died at the hands of the Greek priests who hung him by the neck.) *He was hung by the Greek priests.*

Saint Luke was not a slave. He was Greek and a Gentile. He did become a Roman citizen. He did study medicine at Tarsus and met Paul there. Luke did write some of Acts, not entirely, and there is much interpretation. He was a skilled artist.

The Ultimate Experience
SAINT LUKE, THE PHYSICIAN

We know that you are thinking of presenting our book to your Wednesday group. We wish for you to wait, even though this information is coming out on the Internet. We wish for you to wait for now, for there are people in that group who are not ready to hear this—it is not their timing. As far as the new young man who is drawn to study for the ministry, it would not be doing him a service to bring this information to him at this time. He is a precious soul, very gentle, honest, and loving. He will make a fine minister someday. Whether he preaches about the crucifixion or not, it makes no difference at this time. When it is correct for him, he will change his belief structure. However, for now, as you have sensed, it would be cruel to blast open his beliefs with these new ideas. If you did this, you would be taking away his purpose. You would have him questioning his vocation. He has been called to do this and this he must do. He is to be a Disciple of God. He is to work with the youth and bring them to God. If he tells them about me and my dying on the cross, it is all right. That information will change some day, but probably not for a few generations. You are the forerunner in this. You are to bring forth this information and anchor it and then wait. Wait until the timing says that now it can be released. This book may never be released.

That is all I wish to say, dear one. Type this up now and make your corrections. We will call your next chapter, **The Definitive Commentaries**. *I will bring in an aspect of me that fulfills the intellectual capacity of you. With that, we will leave you to your work. Enjoy! (I do!) We know you do.* **I AM Yeshua**

(2012, David Wilcock is an aspect of Edgar Cayce.)

145

DEFINITIVE COMMENTARIES

*Our dearest one, we are here to work on our book once more. It is coming along very well and we are most pleased. As per your request, you wanted a more definitive commentary for this new chapter, did you not? (*Yes, please, Lord, for there is still some confusion in my mind, so there would be in the minds of Readers also, I think.*) We understand. Therefore, let us see what we can do. You wished for a more intellectual aspect of me.*

I AM Sananda. I have come this morning in order to give a more educational view of the Realities. There are many realities and each has its own perspective. The reality that the crucifixion was in was orchestrated, for it was decided by God and Us that something needed to change in the human mind. Humanity was not advancing as swiftly as God would have wished. It seemed to have met a stalemate.

God brought the Jews out of Egypt. He brought them to Israel, settled the Tribes, and then there were great wars where conquered Tribes became divided and dispersed. They were not meant to be in that land forever. They were meant to carry forth new teachings. Consequently, God sent the man you called *Jesus* in order to help raise the vibratory rate of his people. That was one reality.

Keep in mind, Readers, that that ancient reality was still in the lower dimensions. The people were in the lower third dimension where awareness had not advanced. Hence, Jesus was sent to help raise the vibratory rate. Actually his energy did that. He walked almost every foot of that land. What he was doing was dispersing Light codes throughout the land. One could say he left Light codes with each footprint in the sand. Everyone he spoke to received more Light.

He was not always conscious of doing this. He was not conscious of the fact that there were legions of angels behind him, for he carried a great energy field. Sometimes he was aware of this and at other times he was not. He was a human Being. However, on a spiritual level, he was dispersing Light with every step he took and with every Word he spoke. In that Light was Love, for that is what Light is. It is Love. Everything he said, he said in Light and Love. Even when he was frustrated with the Rabbis, noticing the density they carried and their unopened hearts, he spoke to them with love.

Readers, if you associate Love with being of the gooey kind that is not the correct interpretation of love. Love is passionate; it is Truth; it is kindness; it is empathy; it is conscious; it is aware; it is caring and it can be firm. You hear that expression of *tough love* all of the time. One could say that Jesus was dispersing *tough love* when he was confronting the Rabbis and the priests in the synagogue. That was his purpose.

If you have learned nothing more from this book than that he was dispersing Love and Light to help change the molecular structure of humanity, you have learned well. That was physical reality going on. **He actually was a physical human Being physically walking the Earth.** (We have asked the author to put that in bold print, with spaces staccato-like.) That was the **physical reality**.

Now people may be wondering about the **virtual reality, the hologram**. That was another reality that was prepared by God and Us. (You have often heard that I, Sananda, am the Higher Aspect of Yeshua, your Jesus—your Emanuel.) **That virtual reality was created in order to shock humanity**. How many times have you noticed when something dreadful happens how it pulls the country together? This country of America had its 9/11, the tragedies of the Twin Towers in New York City. We will not go into who was at fault, for there are rumors about that one too, about it being virtual reality. We will let you think about that—that atrocity ought never to have happened. We may speak about that at another time.

However, **this book is about the *Realities of the Crucifixion*.** It was set up that Jesus would rise into a different dimension with our help. I am going to give you a hypothetical question here. **Do you think it might be possible that Jesus was merely lifted onto his spaceship, the Bethlehem Star, and from there created a hologram, a virtual reality that was the crucifixion?** Can you understand that one, Readers? Spaceships have that ability all of the time, to project onto the Earth something that looks real and is not. It is not real. It is a hologram with the components of a person that are brought together in a picture form, similar to gathering parts of an x-ray and making a picture out of them that moves.

Those of you who like to play video games on your iPods are looking at virtual reality. On your television, they use computers to make a baby for the baby scenes, for it might be dangerous for a real baby actor. They have the baby in virtual reality. It is not a real baby, but only looks like one, for it is the computer with the virtual reality. That is what we did on the Bethlehem Star. We made a hologram, a virtual reality of Jesus and placed him in Gethsemane, so that when the soldiers came to take him away, which they did, they took a hologram of your Lord instead.

I will again reiterate that **Judas did not betray Jesus, for Jesus asked him to be part of this play.** Jesus said to him, *go to the soldiers and bring them back to me.* It was the scribes or church fathers or all the other stories that said that Judas had betrayed him for thirty pieces of silver. That is utter nonsense, utter nonsense. Judas was a wealthy man in his own right. He did not have to sell out a friend in order to get thirty pieces of silver, which was nothing compared to what he had stashed away in his own home (*smile*).

Therefore, **you had one reality of Jesus walking the land**, dispersing his Light codes—one reality. **You have a second reality where he is a hologram**—virtual reality, the hologram, just like in television, in the movies, and in your iPods. **Then you have a third reality where none of it happened.** None of it happened because the realities were now coming from the fifth dimension, just as this author is writing her book that we are giving her from the higher fifth into the sixth dimension. **When you get that high in dimensions, in consciousness, in awareness, then none of those atrocities could happen**.

One can never prophesize what the outcome of humanity's free will may be. What was supposed to have happened in order to bring humanity into a higher dimension was that they would be so shocked with the crucifixion that they would change their ways. They were to rise above all of that and come together as a unified force, question their beliefs, question their ways, and change. Grief brings people together. The astonishing aftermath was that it had the **opposite** effect! People focused on the crucifixion and not on his life as it was when they knew him. The scribes, Rabbis, and everyone put words into his mouth. What did he say when he was on the cross. What was going on? Where were Mother Mary and Mary Magdalene and the others who were there? What were they thinking? There were so many projections, so many ways of describing it. It was not realism. They were describing a **hologram**. You play your games and afterwards you describe it as if it were real. That is what they were doing. In a sense, one could say in an amused way, *they killed or thought they had killed a hologram! They had crucified a hologram (smile).*

Now, there is Anna's book that has been written that tells how they brought the body to Joseph of Arimethea's tomb—his private tomb. That did happen. **The hologram body was brought there.** They cleaned it up, left and that body was brought back to the ship, shall we say. It was not real. It was not real. **Your real Jesus was there in the ship.*** That is why he was able to be outside of the tomb. There are all manner of stories how the angels moved the huge stone—all stories, all stories. He was with his ship and came down from the ship

When he appeared to his mother and his wife (and I will say his wife, Mary Magdalene, even though that always shocks people, for they do not want to think of him as ever having been married. They can marry but would not allow him to marry.), he appeared as he looked while he was walking the Earth. He was there a while and that was the other reality. **Those realities had commingled!**

There are people who are living on your planet still in the jungles around Venezuela and the Aborigines in Australia. There are peoples, Indigenous peoples to the planet, very wise people, who have never seen television, and they would not be able to put into words what they were viewing. They have no vocabulary for it. They would call a person who they saw moving and talking on the television screen a god. They would not understand it. Therefore, in a way, you Readers now are trying to understand the virtual reality that took place 2000+ years ago. **These three realities commingled, like Interstate highways on a freeway, coming through each other and out the other side.** People could not differentiate.

Unfortunately, instead of being the positive thing for changing people's beliefs and bringing them together, the different parts of the scenes were made Holy. We spoke about this before in the other chapters—the Stations of the Cross, where he fell down; the blood that he shed when he was nailed—all virtual reality. It was not real. They have made so much of it symbolic. They have taken it as being true. They have taken a virtual reality and said this is Truth. Then Christianity stemmed from that on a crooked path, especially when the church fathers got hold of it.

We have mentioned in other books that Jesus was not the only one to have brought a new consciousness to Earth—the *four pillars,* they were called. The others were killed, but Jesus decided to keep going, keep going. There are people who do not understand that decision either. It is one of *something is better than nothing,* for it would be years—it has taken 2000 years now—it would be years, eons before something like that would happen again to change the energies. Actually, it will never happen again—it will never be replicated. You are living in a different era. It will not be replicated.

The Ultimate Experience
DEFINITIVE COMMENTARIES

Of course, as we have said, many questions will arise from all of this. Everything is turned upside down. It will be generations before it can all be sorted out. We have started to take steps now to bring this to humanity's attention. It is starting to come out on the Internet. It will be in this book and our following books. We keep hammering away at it. Bit by bit companies will stop making crosses in an incorrect way with an emaciated Jesus hanging on them. Churches that will be destroyed from natural causes—Earth changes—and the new ones rebuilt will be built with the glory of Jesus, but not so much of the cross, unless it is a cross that has equal arms. We have spoken of this before—Heaven and Earth as one. There is so much involved—all of your theological schools must change their thinking. Do you think this will happen in the next decade? NO. Young ministers who are being called to work for God to help the young people still will have their vocations. They still will have their strong pull to be God's spokesperson. However, they will be drawn to different churches that have a more open mind. Many of the old dogmas will die out.

Just as King James who was the Disciple James, the brother of Jesus, brought the books of Teachings into a more readable form—the King James Version—someone will have the task of starting a new Bible with new concepts. There will have to be another Master who walks the Earth. It could very well be the Lord Maitreya, the World Teacher. Someone will have to put together all of his Teachings and start a new Bible. Will this be done in your generation? NO. The present generation will have to die out—maybe the next two generations before something new can happen.

If you travel far enough on the continuum and you are in Nirvana, you can look it up in the Library. You will see where there will be a new Bible, for people must always have a spiritual Book that brings them hope, solace, love, and moral teachings. The Book will carry more of the Truth. It will have Genesis, but the mistakes will be corrected and teach more of the Truth. It still will be about Jesus, but will have the Teachings that are Truth. The Book will not speak about the crucifixion, for that will no longer be necessary. That can go into mythology, into mythology where there are the gods—Zeus in the sky, and Athena on the ground. The crucifixion of Jesus can be in mythology. Generations from now can debate; *do you think that was ever true?* There will be fewer people to think that it was true. *Did Zeus ever throw his bolts of thunder at humanity?* It will be in that category. It will never be forgotten, for history is forever written indelibly in the Books of Nirvana.

Therefore, Readers, I hope this has brought some clarification for you. There will be another book. We know what it will be about, but this author does not. It is too soon to say so. We will continue to bring in different aspects of those great Souls that you recognize. Since this book is about the crucifixion, that reality, we will keep bringing in some of the major characters of your Bible. However, for now, dear ones, I will close and let another one say a few words.

I AM the Lord Sananda—the higher aspect of your Lord Yeshua.

Good morning, dear Readers, **I am Mother Mary.** I have come to help soothe any ruffled feathers of the children of my flock. It is always such a shock to hear of new theories, new interpretations, is it not? My precious son, Yeshua, indeed walked the land. His energy is still there, actually. That is why people are drawn to his sacred sites. Many of the churches believe that this is where he was born, this is where he died, and they build their churches on those sites covering up where he was truly born. Did he die in the land you call *Israel?* No, my beloved children, he did not. He is not entombed in that land. He had another land that he was called to where many of your great Avatars go. I am speaking of India, dear ones. He died in India. He did not take his body with him. He simply left it there and it was quietly buried. He arose swiftly back to his God.

The Ultimate Experience
DEFINITIVE COMMENTARIES

There has been much theorizing about all that has taken place. I wanted to assure you Readers that I am not a hologram; I am not an apparition. I am real—very much real. I held my precious baby in my arms—a very real mother with a very real child. Did I kneel at that cross? It all depends what reality you are in, my precious children *(smile)*. It is confusing, is it not? **Physically, I was there with our Lord. When my son was on the cross as a hologram, I was not there. I knew it was not real**.

The dear entity, Anna, who wrote that magnificent book, *Anna, Grandmother of Jesus,* describes all of us. She chose to interweave the story of the virtual reality with the physical reality. She wove them together. You can approach her book like the Da Vinci Code, for it is a magnificent piece of writing. Claire Heartsong is a superb channel. This is where you can come into your own discernment, Readers, and ask yourself what part of that book—we call it the *Anna Book*—is in the real physical reality and what part of the book was she writing about virtual reality. Interesting, is it not, where the realities are so commingled that you cannot tell them apart!

This is happening in your present life all the time. You have heard where life is an illusion, so start thinking of it in that way. **The only reality is of you as a soul in your human body on Earth in a physical way, the caretaker of Earth.** You as a soul came in with a purpose, so it is hoped that you are performing your purpose. Just ask in what reality are the stories that your government puts out—the stories that the media are told to write whether they believe them or not. Many times, it is not the Truth, as you are beginning to know.

The whole 9/11 story of the Twin Towers is not the Truth, as some of you are beginning to suspect. For the many who were killed, that certainly was true for them, but that was their purpose—the way they chose to die. You certainly can have compassion for the families who experience that grief. However, those who died are quite happy. Many already have come back into other bodies, for they had served their purpose. They had followed

153

whatever it was they were supposed to do and experienced the death they had chosen, and now they have a new life.

Therefore, dear Readers, keep an open mind; allow these new ideas to percolate; allow these new ideas to germinate, to stimulate you, so that perhaps other ideas can now come forth. Any new concept, new theory, new history is always a jolt to a person. It is, to use your expression, a *heads up*! This is what we are doing in this book. It is *heads up time* for you Readers. Many people will not finish this book. Many people will not be led to buy this book. This book may never be published, but only sold as a manuscript to those who have heard about it. That too then, becomes the purpose, for **it is important that these words be put on paper. It anchors the energy**, you see. It anchors it. In a way, it seals it.

All right, our dear ones, I am always with you. Please call upon me. I am not an apparition for you. I am with you always, even though you cannot see me. I bless you, my children.

I AM Mother Mary.

*The Lord Sananda-Yeshua has his own space ship called the *Bethlehem Star*. The light from that ship is what people saw in the sky during Jesus' birth. It was from this ship that the hologram during the Crucifixion manifested. A space ship also led Moses and Joshua (Jesus) and the Hebrews for 40 years across the desert, feeding them manna.

(Author: I was tempted to delete the part about the space ship and the hologram. It seemed too much of a stretch for even me. However, my guidance said to leave it in. So we can agonize over this possibility in the chapter together!)

SAINT PETER

*Good morning, our dear one, back to continue our book and since your time is somewhat limited this morning, we will see what we can do in forty-five minutes. (*Thank you, Yeshua.*) What I wish to do this morning is to bring forth another speaker, one who you have not channeled for this book, but one who is very much a part of that whole Biblical era. It is a male figure and one of my Disciples, of course (smile).*

Hello to this channel and to the Readers, **I AM Peter**, the one that the Bible says denied the Lord three times before the cock crowed. Well, I hate to tell you, Readers, for you have had your balloons popped so much that I am afraid here is another balloon to pop (*laughter*), but **I never denied your Lord—never!** Oh, my goodness, I ask who could not love him who knew him, for he was a wonderful soul, wonderful friend, and a wonderful Teacher. I do not have the superlatives enough in my vocabulary to tell you about him.

It was also written that I was jealous because Mariam and Mary Magdalene were teaching. I would like to put that in perspective. You use in your modern day the terms *jealous or jealousy*. I would say that there **was** a dynamic there, for it touched upon the fact that we were males born into a patriarchal society, programmed by our parents on how a male ought to act, how to receive from other males, to be kind, but to know that you are always the boss. You are supposed to be the head of your family. What **you** said was the family rule and we practiced that.

Therefore, when this young man came into our midst with such charisma that you could not help but follow him, it was difficult for me (and from now on I will just talk about myself, but it was for the rest of the Disciples also) to give the women their due. These very learned women were extremely aware for their age, for they were both young. To allow them to give the correct interpretation of what our Master was telling us went against my male ego.

Some of you may be wondering how we addressed your Jesus. The Bible has us calling him *Master* all of the time. It was not until he was near to leaving the country that we gave him the title of *Master*, for up to that time we would call him *Rabbi*. As we got to know him more, we would say *Yeshua. Hey, Yeshua, tell me about this; I just don't get it.* Yeshua with a twinkle in his eye would give us another parable to chew upon (*smile*). Oh my gosh, we would say *here he goes again!* He was forever tweaking our intellectual side to get us to think, to get us to figure out the morals of the stories—the kernels of the parables.

Some of the stories that the Bible state are accurate; however, it was difficult for me to accept these women who were quite lovely in their own right, as having the ability to understand Yeshua's words better than we. We did not speak much about women's intuition, energies, chakras, and things of that nature. We did not think in those terms. We did not think of egos and a person's awareness. They were not our terms. Our terms were more for the common folks that we were. Since Yeshua spoke in Aramaic, there would be many interpretations of a single word.

Yeshua had a commanding voice. I now recognize that there was energy in his voice that came forth. It had a force behind it that could just enter into you, like a piercing arrow of Truth. Many times when he talked to me, I would get goose bumps. You might say that *it made your hair stand on end.* I did not understand it. I did not understand the force of energy that he carried. That same force was not only full of strength, but it was full of Love. **He was so full of Love!**

If we had any kind of a personal problem, and many of us did, just as in modern times with a family member, etcetera, we would take it to him. He would never take sides, but he would give us another little story, a parable, that would light up for us where the problem lay. As I look back, he was teaching us the *equality of women*. He treated all of us with gentleness and respect, thanking us many times, thanking us for being his companions.

He was so dedicated to his purpose in life as a Teacher. I now know that that purpose came from God. He had work to do, not only in Israel but also in foreign countries. He was not meant to be in Israel into old age. He was to shed his Light codes, or more aptly put, to give forth his Light and Love to humanity.

To get back to Mariam and Mary Magdalene who were strong women in their own right, I now can see how they too struggled with their purpose in life. Mary Magdalene of course was Yeshua's bride by this time. I do not know why the scribes did not write this. It was no secret. Rabbis were meant to marry. They always married. He married later than most, actually. With Mariam, one could see that there was a special bond between brother and sister. Mariam's husband, Nathaniel/Bartholomew, often accompanied her, as did their son, Benjamin. Most of this was never written. It is as if the church fathers only took what they wanted to emphasize. The emphasis upon me was to denounce him.

As I look back, the church fathers wanted someone to play the role that they were going to give him. In other words, let one of the men in Yeshua's group say that he did not know Yeshua when the soldiers came to take him away. The church fathers had a whole play similar to directors of a theatrical drama. They put each person in their play to star in a particular role. Mine was to denounce that I ever knew Yeshua. Of course, there was no acquiescence on my part. I never knew about it. They just wrote the script that way and in the same way that they wrote about Judas, none of which is true. Yeshua had asked Judas to lead the soldiers to where he was. He had asked him to do it, for Judas was known among the Roman court. You do not send an unknown person to say that Yeshua wants you to come to him. You send someone they would know. Those were difficult times, Readers. We had much to learn. We were shocked when the soldiers came for Yeshua.

The Ultimate Experience
SAINT PETER

We did not know when he had transformed himself—when he had created the hologram to play that nasty part of the crucifixion. We did not know that. He looked so real, but after **my own death, which was not a pretty sight**, I came to understand what was happening. We were with the Lord—for I shall call him that now—we were with him for just a few years, for it was at the age of thirty-three that he left the country—if you believe in that reality. On the other hand, if you believe in the virtual reality, he was thirty-three when he went to the cross—ah, all the different realities that take place during one's lifetime.

It is also written in the Bible that Peter said *on this rock I will build a church*. Hmmm, where the church fathers came up with that one, I am not sure. You see, after Yeshua left and the Holy Spirit came upon us, we became teachers in our own right. We taught the parables, the teachings, and the concepts that Yeshua had taught us. It was not in my consciousness that I was going to be building a church. All of that stemmed from the stories that the church fathers were putting out. We did not think of Yeshua's Word as being a church. We only had grown up knowing about the synagogue. We did not know that much about Islamic teachings and since there was no Christianity yet, we did not know about that either.

My suggestion, Readers, will be to take the different stories that you have read in the Bible, just like Lord Sananda was telling you yesterday, and think of them as reading mythology. Try not to worry what was real and what was not. Just see them as mythology, for I can say that most of what you read will not be in the true Light. There are too many realities involved. The history of those days has become garbled. For any of you Readers who have gone to Israel and walked where Jesus supposedly walked and visited the different churches that are all built on the various sites where he was supposed to have been, know that his energy **is** still there. Know that he did walk much of that land.

However, if the tour guides say that this is where he fell, take it as a myth, a cruel myth, actually. Most of what is written is not true; most is not true. Please let go of the myth that whenever you hear the cock crow you think that is when Peter denied the Lord (*laughter*). I did not do that; I did not do that (*more laughter*). Those of you Readers who may be well known, bordering on being famous, do you know what is going to be written about you when you have died? A good example of that could be the old-time movie stars who have made their transition to Nirvana and all the various stories that people tell about them. *I knew such and such; this is what he did.* That borders on gossip, actually, and just how accurate is gossip?

You see back in those Biblical times there were many gossipers. There was much gossip, for that was the only way that we knew how to spread the word! We would tell something to someone and they would tell it to someone else, maybe dress it up a little bit. I think you have a term *fish stories*. These were people in the oral tradition carrying on the *fish stories* of the crucifixion.

Many eons later, as I look back at that lifetime, I can see it had many intricacies interwoven. It was a most difficult life for me, a most difficult life. With that, dear Readers, I leave you now.

I AM Saint Peter and I send blessings to all of you.

(Oh, thank you, Saint Peter. That was beautiful, thank you.) *You are welcome, dear child and please forgive me if I did not understand you as Mariam.* (For me, Mariam is like mythology, also, so don't give it another thought, thank you, smile). *Actually, we did come to terms with that and I came to respect you greatly.* (And I, you, I am sure, thank you, Saint Peter.)

*(Saint Peter was Simon ben Jonah or Simon Peter. He was born in Bethsaida. It is purported that he was crucified upside down per his request in Rome during Nero's Persecution. This is what he was referring to when he stated **his death was not a pretty sight**. His major shrine is Saint Peter's Basilica and he is buried there in Vatican City. History gives two dates of his death, June 29 or October 13, ca. 64AD.)*

The Ultimate Experience

MATTHEW the APOSTLE

(This is how I start each channeling in order to assure that I am channeling only the highest of Light: "I now demand in the name of Jesus the Christ to know if you are a Being of the Jesus the Christ Consciousness, if you are a Being of the true God of the God Light Consciousness of the Creator, answer me yes, or no.") *Yes my dear heart, I truly am. I have come once again to work on our book. As you are sensing, we are coming to the close of this. We have put more and more emphasis on the* Realities of the Crucifixion *hoping to awaken people more, hoping they will let go of their misconceptions, what has been taught to them. We hope that by bringing forth the different Apostles and the other Speakers that the people will get in touch more with their own beliefs and know that they may need to be changed, for when you create a belief, it does not necessarily mean you are to have it 'til death do us part (smile). It means you are trying on a suit of clothes. You may wear them for a while and then they become tired and old and it is time to let them go and put on a new suit of clothes. This we are hoping will be accomplished for anyone who finally gets through this book.*

Now you have a few questions about Saint Peter's chapter. (Yes, please, Lord. There are two dates for his death. One is in June, the other is in October, and both are stated to be in the year 64AD.) *The year is correct, June 29, 64AD. He was crucified, and it was his choice to be upside down. I do not think he will do that one again (smile). This was in real time. It was not a hologram. He did this for real.*

Many of your Saints martyred themselves. It seems the way souls wish to die. You have a question in your mind as to whether you were ever crucified in a past life. Of course you were! All souls seem to want this type of death. As we have said before, there is a great learning in death. Souls, as they advance up the ladder, will have a death one way, and the next time they will

160

choose another way; or they may decide a particular way several times. After a while, you will have experienced every way there is to die and then you will just start being pickier. "I think I will die this way. It seemed to be the easiest for me in order to just slip out." (Cancer is one of the easier ways.)

The more advanced you become, you can just leave; you can just leave and pull the cords. Your Monad breaks the silver cord and you are dead. The examiners of bodies many times will just put down "a massive heart attack," for they have no explanation for the death. However, that is for the higher aspects of a person. When you get to that reality, you can just pull your own cords out, sever your own cords, and then leave. That is what I did in India. In Kashmir, I just pulled my own cords and left, for I wished for my body to go back to the Earth in that Hebrew way of dying, "ashes to ashes..."

However, this book is not about that. This book is about the different realities that surrounded the crucifixion, which commingled so intricately that one could not tell reality from illusion from Truth.

Yes, I do know that we will need to write a new Foreword and Introduction or put the two of them together. Therefore, take the two sections and set them aside and we will start afresh, for the tone of this book has changed so much. Do keep the first two chapters of Mariam though, for they are sweet and gentle. It shows a loving time between brother and sister.

This book will be finished in August, 2006. Then do the regular editing and give it to Heather for proofreading, and then get your copyright. It all takes time. Maybe it will be ready to distribute as a manuscript in September. We suggest not rushing into it. Let it settle.

Now this morning... (I do not have another tape handy, so we need to stay within forty-five minutes, smile.) *I suggest you get another tape because it might be longer.* (OK, excuse me, please. I quickly grab another tape, get the wrapping off, and come back. I am concerned, for I may have broken the transmission. However, he picks right up where he left off.)

All right Readers... (This is still Yeshua?) *Yes, dear one, this morning we are going to continue our journey bringing in another Disciple, for there are still several more who wish to speak—who are in line. The one we are bringing in today is Matthew. Matthew had an interesting life and I will let him tell you about it.*

Good morning, Readers, **I AM the Apostle, Matthew**, another one of the Twelve. I have been listening while my Brothers speak—how they saw the different aspects of our journey together. I was younger than the other Apostles were. I was one of the last to join. An inner circle surrounded the Lord, made up of those who had been with him longer. He showed no favorites, but we mentally drew that circle within that group. As with any relationship in a group, there are always just a few who become the inner circle. Then there is the rest of the group who may not have this privilege until they have earned it. One must always earn the privilege of being placed in a group.

I was from the common folk. I had great curiosity. I had a great love for God that was taught to me in the synagogue. I knew no other way. When I heard of this Rabbi, I was drawn to hear him and then drawn to remain with him. In modern times, one could say that God sent me to him, for that was my purpose. I did not know it at that time, but that was my purpose to be one of the Twelve.

Those of you who are familiar with numerology know that *twelve* is quite a Biblical number, for it is used throughout the Universe and in this world. There are twelve months in your calendar year. In the Jewish tradition, a Jewish lad goes into adulthood in his twelfth year. We have the twelve Tribes. Centuries later, we have the twelve Apostles. Twelve seems to be a final number and an important one.

The Ultimate Experience
MATTHEW THE APOSTLE

I was not born into wealth. My family members were simple people, fishermen. My mother worked hard as women did in those days. I had brothers and sisters. Actually, when I left home I merely walked away for I was not drawn to stay. There were other brothers older than I was. Therefore, I did not have the responsibility of the family. I could leave. Sometimes it pays not to be the first-born. I could leave, so I did.

I joined this young band of dedicated souls when I was quite young. Yeshua was probably around twenty-seven or eight. In your modern times, men of that age are just becoming wise. Many are not doing a very good job of it in my opinion (*smile*). We were no different back then. We were not worldly. Remember, without any television, radios, and newspapers, we did not have the news given to us every hour. We would just know local things by word of mouth—as Peter said *fish stories*. We interpreted the *fish stories*. Therefore, we did not always know what was going on in the world. We did not know what was going on with our government—only through the *fish stories*.

I was there for part of that reality. I was part of the hologram reality. I knew no different when the soldiers came and led Yeshua away. We were never told that Judas betrayed him. That is a complete fabrication. We were told that Yeshua had asked Judas to bring the soldiers back to him. Now he could have gone to them, but he needed the time to go back to his ship, the Bethlehem Star, and create the hologram. That can be so real that the only way that you would know would be to look into his eyes and find that there was not a soul there. It would be like looking into the eyes of a live doll that walked, talked, and could bleed.

I do not know what all was told about me. Probably most of it is someone else's idea of what took place. However, the Holy Spirit came upon me with such force that I was knocked out of my body for several hours. The Bible portrays it as being a soft transformation. It was not. It was powerful. I was taken out of my body and up into the higher realms and shown what I was to do. I was to write the Words of the Master to the best of my ability.

The Ultimate Experience
MATTHEW THE APOSTLE

I was to teach. I did not have the education to be a great teacher, but the Holy Spirit enlarged our energy fields so that if you were near our fields, you would be magnetized to come to us. Whether people listened out of politeness or not, I do not know. We taught the stories of our Lord to the best of our ability. In later years, eons actually, my writings ended up in the New Testament in the Gospels of Matthew, Mark, Luke, and John.

Just like in your modern times, if you take four people and have them describe a certain scene, you will find the framework could be similar, but it is still selective hearing and selective wordage, since each of us had his own experience. What I would remember, someone else would not. What he would remember, I had not written. Therefore, I can see how in later years history would have a difficult time putting our four renditions together. They did not match in many ways.

I do not know why I did not write of the Rabbi's marriage. I do not know, except it was a personal happening and was not part of the Teachings. I wrote about the Teachings. I cannot help but think the other three might have mentioned the marriage and the church fathers removed the information. That is the only explanation I can think of that could be the reason.

I did not live long into old age, but long enough to do what I was supposed to do, for after the Holy Spirit had come upon me, I was shown the path I must take. I was shown my death. I do not know why when people are shown their lives that they must be shown their death also. It was not a pleasant death. Did any of the Twelve experience an easy death? It does not look like it, does it? I was stoned. That is a cruel way to die, but one that was quite common, for then several people would share the guilt and not just one. If men only had had the love that the Master carried in his heart, there would not be any need for these kinds of death. Needless to say that was the last time I did that one!

I am not known for any one particular talent. When we come into a body at birth, we experience the lifetime that we have chosen. At times, it was hard for me that I had chosen that. It would be similar to your being in Heaven setting up a lifetime and then you and your Higher Souls decide with all the other players that there will be a Holy Man, and you are going to be one of the ones who surround him. You are to be one of the ones who follow and act as a shield for him. You will be one of the ones who are more among the public, so that questions would be fielded to you. If you could not answer them, you would turn them over to the Master.

We made quite a sight as we walked along the dusty paths. Can you imagine twelve Apostles tagging along and then hordes of people following us, following him? We would have it pinpointed where we would stay each night. We would have relatives and stay with them. If they did not have room in their house, we would stay in the courtyard. Most people had walled-in courtyards for safety. Within that courtyard, there would be tables set up where they served the food. We could lay our sleeping pallets down and sleep. They would have different sections in the courtyard so that there could be areas for quiet conversation with different people. It was a matter of safety, but it was a time for intimacy that one could have with others—just surrounded by this protective wall of bricks and mud mortar.

I did not dwell on what we were doing particularly. My needs were met; I received my food; I received a place to sleep. I was a nomad at heart. One could say that it fit right in with my lifestyle. There were no movies, television, newspapers, or magazines. Therefore, just walking the towns from one town to the next provided the entertainment for the day. You would meet people along the road; you would talk to them. You would go to the different houses that agreed to have us come. You would be able to bathe in a primitive way, at least to wash the dust off your feet and hands. Some of the Twelve were married and others were not. I was not married at that time, but I did marry and I did have children. I carried on the work of the Lord after he left.

With the virtual reality, these soldiers were on the lookout for the other *rebels,* as they put it, those who would stir up the community and say there was going to be a new king. People carried on their lives. We would gather and talk about Yeshua and wonder what he was doing, how many children he had. We spoke about the normal things that people talk of when they get together. Therefore, in a way, we were carrying on those oral traditions, our *fish stories* that differed from each other. We did not do it on purpose, you see. We believed what we were writing and saying. However, as you know in your games of childhood, *Simon says this and Simon says that,* half the time it was wrong much to the giggles of the participants.

The most difficult time for me came when I was in my thirties, for I had a series of unpleasant experiences. They came as a grouping. I was accused of being a heretic. I was accused of blasphemy. I was accused of being a follower of a cult, for in the early stages of Christianity it was thought of as a *cult*. Therefore, I was looked upon with suspicion. They did not like what I was doing, which to my mind was merely minding my own business. I pondered long and hard over many of the parables wishing that Yeshua were there so I could ask him what that meant. *Tell me again, Lord, what does this mean? Tell me again, Lord, about the Kingdom of God. Tell me again, Lord, about the afterlife. Tell me again, Lord, will I ever see God? Tell me again, Lord, will I ever see you again?* All of these questions came up. He was gone and no one was there to answer them. Everyone was just as perplexed. We did the best that we could; we did the best we could.

After the crucifixion and the holographic scene, I was stunned, for I had believed it! The nails going into his hands and feet were as if nails were going through mine. I felt such a loss, such a loss. There came a point in my life when I did not care. I did not want to live. I was afraid to die, but my solace had left. I had no one to rely upon but myself. It was a dark time for me. People tried to help in any way that they could, but it was a struggle in my mind. Oh, how I missed his counsel. He was so clear. He was such a guiding Light in my life. When he left in whatever way that you think he left, Reader—whether in virtual reality, or he left the country, or it never happened, whatever way your belief is about how he left—I was inconsolable. I left the others for a while, lost touch somewhat as each went his separate way. Therefore, I started writing and started remembering everything I could about those years, those happy years, how we joined him, what he said. That helped me; that helped.

Did I write everything accurately? Probably not, but I wrote as accurately as I could. Remember that *selective hearing*. What I remembered, I wrote. Therefore, dear Readers, one more of the Disciples comes to you and tells you of his experiences. I felt when the Lord left that he had taken half of my life with him. I had forgotten that this was the way it was supposed to be. I had forgotten while in Nirvana that I would be with him only for a short time and then he was to go on. I had forgotten I had agreed to carry on with my mission to help anchor his energy and that I was to write the Lord's Parables and Teachings. Those were dark days for me, and I feel that the rendition I wrote tells some of that.

Therefore, Readers, with that I will close. Just know that to some people it might sound so glamorous to be a Disciple, or an Apostle, or a follower of Jesus, hither and yon. However, to put it in perspective, it was only wonderful while he was there. After he left, we had our personal *hells* to deal with. We had to practice what we preached. You see, they did not have psychological counselors back then. Yeshua in his clarity was our Counselor and Teacher. It would be like in your life when your counselor or therapist leaves. It feels like such a loss. We need help to process our own issues. There was no one to turn to. Therefore, we processed our own issues to the best of our ability; we talked to God; but it was not easy; it was not easy for me. Therefore, Readers, I have given you a different perspective. As I was saying, it sounds glamorous to have been an Apostle, but so many of us were martyred for our dedication. Would I do it all over again if I had the chance? Well, at this level of clarity, I would, but only if the Father is sending me. This is not a task a soul would take on lightly. This task was given to you by God. I now understand that; I understand that.

With that, I leave you, Readers, and thank you for the privilege of speaking with you today. I bless you; **I AM Matthew, the Apostle**. *(*Thank you, Lord.*)* You are welcome, child. You were there also, you know. (Yes, but I know little of what I did.*)* You played a large part in that play, a large part that few of us have acknowledged. I did not write about you and for this, I regret; this I regret. I will step aside now. Adieu.

*I see that you have some questions for us. (*Yes, please, Lord, for after Saint Matthew gave me his message, there are different things that came up. I do not know if he was giving us a different perspective, or did he actually have great grief and psychological loss because he missed you so much.) *He was one of the younger Apostles, so that in a sense he did not have the maturity that the others had. Therefore, he did miss me greatly when I left.*

*(*He was the son of Alpheus who was a fisherman, or what **did** he do?) *He mainly fished. That is what he did. You know Matthew was a tax collector and not very favorably looked upon by his brethren—the brothers and sisters in his family. It was a way for him to make money. That is where I saw him. The story goes that I asked him to follow me. That is not quite accurate, for Matthew asked if he could join us. He had seen the other men with me. He did not like his job that much, so he asked if he could join us. He was quite an adventurer and liked traveling around, as he has said.*

(History is not clear where he died. Some say it was in Ethiopia, south of the Caspian Sea, not the one in Africa. Matthew said that he was stoned to death—a martyr's death.) *He did have a martyr's death, and he was stoned in the Ethiopian area. All of that is true.*

*(*They also called him, Levi—Matthew-Levi.) *Yes, that is one of his names. Many times the Jews had two names, so he was Matthew-Levi. Sometimes he was just called Levi.*

*(*He also said that he was one of the last Disciples to have joined you.) *Yes, that is correct.*

*(*Did you tell any of the Apostles, ones who were closest to you, that you were going to enact a hologram? He acted as if he did not know about it.) *I told only one other person. I told John what I was going to do. Therefore, John seemed not to have taken that much of an interest in the crucifixion, for he knew it was not real.*

*(*History does not tell how old Matthew was when he died.) *He did die young. I believe he was only in his forties. I do not believe that he reached fifty. He did marry after I left and had children, but it was not a very happy life. He struggled with his maturity and writing the journeys down helped him. He was a good writer in that he was descriptive. He told you that he was being as accurate as he possibly could be.*

Now, I think we have covered Matthew really well and if you are up for it, we will continue with the next chapter, for we are not quite finished with the book. You have approximately one ninety-seven or eight pages. We are not quite finished yet. I do like the way we have set this up. There is the channeling; then as the questions come up, we clarify them for the Readers. It is very good. They are starting to get some Truth as to what happened with the Apostles. This is good. Now let us commence the next chapter.

The Ultimate Experience

MARY MAGDALENE

*We are going to bring back one of the women, for my beloved
has not spoken for a while in this book. You know she was very
much a part of my life. We were married and actually Matthew
does not say that he wrote about my marriage, but the others did.
I believe it might have been Mark who did, but his description
of the wedding was removed by the church fathers. Therefore, it
never came out, but one of those four did write something about
our marriage. Without further comments from me, let us bring
forth my beloved who is still my beloved, by the way. She is my
twin flame; she is the other half of me, the Light of my life. I will
step back now.*

*(*I was late in sitting this morning, for I was transcribing
the tape. Is this a problem for you? I know you can bi-locate all
over the place, but I did not know if you need an exact time to
meet with me.) *You play your CD and then I come; I come. No,
it is all right. This is our agreement. I overshadow you, as Saint
Germain has told you. Therefore, when you are in place, that is
our contract; that is our agreement, and I will come. Sometimes
it takes a little longer than other times, but such is life on my side
(smile). All right dear one, let us have my beloved come forth.*

Good morning, to our dear Readers and this precious channel,
my friend, my friend Mariam who is now in another body. We did
have some great times together. **I AM Mary Magdalene.** As the
book has proceeded, the secret is out that there were these three
realities commingled. We led you to this fact one step at a time,
bit by bit, for it never pays to dump the whole story, the whole
concept, onto someone. It is too overwhelming. Therefore, we
have brought you forth slowly, and we hope it has not been too
much of a painful journey for you.

Of course I knew my Lord—and I call him that as an endearing
term—my Lord, the Lord of my heart—he was half of me, you

see, so I knew what he was up to. I agreed whole-heartedly, for the Romans were getting very nasty in the way they were treating people. It was from fear, you know. Fear brings out the worst in people. Therefore, it was in that fear mode that they started to be more aggressive when they warned him. They did beat him. It was not an enjoyable sight for me as I helped put salve on his wounds and washed the blood off his body. It did take him several days to recover, for the wounds were quite deep. However, he knew how to heal his body and I too was a healer, so that with the two of us working together, we soon had him up and about.

Now back to the virtual reality—I knew he was going to do this. I heartedly agreed. I told only his Mother and Mariam, my friend. He told John. We understood this, you see. We understood how one creates a hologram. We were able to do this in Egypt where we studied, and we did this somewhat when we were at Mount Carmel with the Essenes. Therefore, it was not an unusual concept for us, but certainly one that saved his life.

Recently, they had a movie on television that this channel was watching. It showed a virtual reality where you put the headgear on and that would project out for you. It projected the two people onto a seaside, a beach. One of them took up a shell and rasped it across his chest, drawing blood. You saw the blood. Then in the next scene, they were back in the studio, took the helmets off, and there was no blood on his chest. That is what virtual reality is like. You create something that is not real. Yeshua created this using the technology that was on board the ship, The Bethlehem Star. However, even though you have a virtual reality going on, there are people who do not know that it is not real. Therefore, you must be careful. You must remain in seclusion, which we did. We stayed very much in the background, for everything was an illusion, and we were not going to get caught up in it. Interestingly enough, there is still emotion attached to that, because we picked up the emotions from the other people. We could feel their fear, their anguish, and their curiosity. No one was gleeful, thank God. Soldiers looked on and did their duty. You know when you are in the military you do your duty. You are told to do this and you do it. That is that way of life that you have chosen. Therefore, they did their duty.

I prefer the reality in the higher dimensions, the fifth reality where nothing happened. He still was whipped, but then we left. Therefore, no crucifixion took place. That scene surely was the better reality. Humanity in that lower dimension wanted a crucifixion. The priests in that lower dimension wanted to get rid of Yeshua in any way that they could. They followed their Laws. They were very careful about that. Nevertheless, if they could malign him in some way and get the Romans to sentence him, then their hands were clean. It was greed; it was mob mentality. It was the dark forces coming forward. Everything needed to be transmuted. People were playing their roles, their pre-birth agreements. All of that was going on in the attempt to raise people's consciousness. God so wanted His people to raise their consciousness and get away from killing each other just because one person does not think the way that **the other person thinks** he ought to. Those were such dark days.

Those of us who are part of history come in knowing it will be a dark life. However, we did not expect it to be **that** dark. It always takes a soul by surprise, I think. The true joy in my life, of course, was marrying the love of my life and having our children. That brought great joy to me. I also missed the people I had to leave behind—the Marys, my Aunt Mary, my best friend Mariam. We had fun with their names.

There is not a great deal one can add. The various scenes were played out and written about in history. It is written that I went to France. I took my children there. Actually we went there as a family. We were many years in Egypt. We were many years in India. Then we went to France. It was there that Yeshua and I agreed to carry on our lives and our life work and not be together. It was a wrenching of my heart when he left, for he had a pulling, you see. He knew that he needed to travel more.

The Ultimate Experience
MARY MAGDALENE

He traveled to the Himalayas and back into India, and I stayed in France and journeyed throughout that area and raised our children. You have a bit of that history with the fact that our bloodline was combined with the French royalty. It is interesting that Saint Germain was so prominent in royal circles, trying to save Marie Antoinette from being beheaded, but they would not listen to him. Here are these souls. Saint Germain was Joseph, the father of Yeshua. Joseph made his transition in the Himalayas and then came back as Saint Germain, as he was called. He carried that genetic line, those codes. Yeshua then carried those codes and we gave them to our children. The children married into those Royal lines—carried on the lineage.

It is an interesting thought that when someone has what we will call a famous life in one area—and I am thinking of Yeshua and myself, Mary Magdalene—people put you in a box and expect you to stay there. This is similar to Mariam's and Yeshua's little pet bug fort. They put you in a fort and expect you to stay there. Then they were shocked—they would not believe *you did not stay there?* No, we left the country. We did not stay there. We traveled. We were in Egypt. We were in India. We were in Europe, spreading our codes, doing our work, teaching the equality of women, which did not go over very big (*smile*). Nevertheless, we tried.

It is written that I came over to France in a boat from Alexandria that Joseph of Arimethea provided. That was one reality, but the real one was that I was with Yeshua. We traveled together. There was no boat and there was no storm. There is supposed to be a cave in France. I was there. You would be surprised, Readers, how many people used caves. It was in our blood; we were brought up that way. In Qumran in Israel, there are caves all over that area. Maybe it stems from the cave dwellers. I do not know.

However, when there was a large cave, many times we would make that into a grotto or chapel. We would worship. Many people would make them into shrines and use the Goddess energy. Consequently, it was not unusual to have a cave that

The Ultimate Experience
MARY MAGDALENE

Mary Magdalene was supposed to have lived in. Caves are very comfortable. They are cool in summer, and with fires, they are quite warm in winter. They keep you out of the wind, rain, and the snow. With furs to lie on and cover you, you were warm. In those days having furs to walk or lie on from deer and foxes and the more exotic animals, such as the mink, was not considered a horrible act. There were many rabbits; you ate the meat and saved the skins. You sewed them together and they provided warmth.

Caves also provided an environment where you were away from the density of cities or too many people crowded into small areas, like a house with all the relatives in three rooms. It was too close. You were not clean. Therefore, much of what is written about my being in Europe in the cave is true. Now it is said I died there in the cave. That is also true.

It is written that I was with our Lord when he died in Kashmir, for he was going to ascend and I was to be there. That is not true. By this time, we were able to bi-locate, so that I was able to go to him whenever I wished and he would come to me. Now these would be in our private moments, and no one would know about them but us. Nevertheless, I knew when it was his time. He had fulfilled all that he had needed to fulfill. It was time for him to leave and so he did. However, I was not with him.

In my own cave, I did much the same thing, for I have told you that we are one. I was not going to live for years after he had died. He died at a ripe old age, seventy-nine, or so. I was considered an old *sage.* I taught about the Goddess energies, the feminine aspects of people. When I felt that it was time for me to ascend, that is what I did. I left my body and went right to God and to my Love, right into his arms, actually. It was agreed that he would go first and in that way he could greet me when I came. We had a grand reunion. Oh, wow, did we have things to talk about—a grand reunion.

Therefore, our dear Readers, we are at the end of our journey with you also. I will probably come back once more and make a closing statement, if we are going to do that with this book. I do not know. However, it has been my pleasure to be with you. Know that you can talk with me. You can ask me to come. I would be happy to do that.

It is a very simple matter for me. With that, I will close now with my blessings.

I AM Mary Magdalene.

(Thank you, Lady.) *You are welcome my dear friend, my dearest friend. What a grand time we had, always talking about Yeshua. What a grand time, adieu for now.* (Thank you, thank you, Mary.)

Commentaries: Good morning our dear soul, I AM Yeshua back once again. You have questions for me, I see. (Yes, Lord, I have just finished typing up Mary Magdalene's chapter. She mentioned some things I had heard before, but I wanted the validation, if I may.) *Of course, dear one, we are always happy to do that.*

(It is written that she went by boat that Joseph of Arimethea had obtained in Alexandria, Egypt, and that they had a stormy passage to France and just barely made it. Your comments, please.) *There was no boat. That was not the reality that we were in. That was another reality that Anna had commingled. That is sufficient to say.*

(She said that you went to France as a family.) *Yes, we did; we journeyed with our whole family to France. Actually, we had more children who were born in France.*

(Your children married into the French royalty as they grew up?) *Yes, one of the boys married one of the Princesses of that Merovingian family. That is what The Da Vinci Code said that upset so many people. That is on the Internet and is all true.*

(She states that you two separated in France, as you had things to do, so she raised the children. Would you go into the reason for the separation, if I am not being too personal here?) *Dear one, that is such history that there is nothing to be personal about (laughingly). Yes, Mary and I had our work to carry on.*

The Ultimate Experience
MARY MAGDALENE

She had to stay there, for she was anchoring a particular energy into that area. She was carrying the Goddess energies, as you know, and had to anchor that energy there, as well as spread the Light codes.

In the meantime, I was called to go to the Himalayas for some more teachings. I did not stay there per se, but traveled back and forth into India and round about. The reasoning was that she needed to do her work, anchoring the energies for that whole area, and I needed to do mine. In the Himalayas and in that whole area, I also was anchoring energies. I talked about the Teachings. One could say I was bringing in Christianity to that whole area. I did not think of it as being Christianity as much as it being the Truth of God and the Light that I was carrying. Next question.

(Some writers say that she was with you at the time of your death. Is that correct?) *No, it is not. She was not with me in flesh, but was with me in Spirit, for she knew what was going to happen. I have told you that I just left my body and she knew that. My age is not important, but I was an old man, an old man. (*It has been said that you were 79.*) That is close enough. I was considered an old man in those days. My mission was finished. I do not know if it was totally accomplished, but it was finished.*

(When Mary Magdalene died, did she die in a cave?) *Yes, and there were people around her. Our children, actually, were with her, for she had asked them to come. Therefore, she did not die alone, while I chose to do that. I just went into a meditative state and left. She chose to have her family there. She too was able to bless them and then left—no illness, no debilitating disease. She just left the children and came into my arms. It was wonderful (smile).* (And what would her age have been?) *She was just about my age. She was a senior; let's put it that way—a wise, gentle senior. She had her wrinkles, her gray hair, but I saw her beauty shining through those wonderful eyes.*

(I have no further queries from this chapter. Do you wish to add anything more?) *No, dear one, but I would caution* the Readers that if you go to the Internet to read up on Mary Magdalene or any of the other Apostles, know that much of it has come from the Catholic Church and to be conscious of that fact and not take everything verbatim, for it is not entirely accurate. They will never tell you that Mary Magdalene was married and had children. Therefore, just be wary of what you read on the Internet.

All right, dear one let us call it a day. The next time I speak, we will go back, bring in some of the different Contributors to this book, and rewrite the Introduction. That will be a long transmission, so I did not want to bring it in this morning after we have already talked for a while. Therefore, if you have no further questions—(no, thank you, Lord). You are welcome, dear one. We will be back. (Thank you, I hope so, smile.) Over and out with love, **I AM Yeshua.**

SECTION 3—Closing Statements

CLOSING STATEMENTS

I AM Yeshua-Sananda. I come to you this day in order to give a closing statement for this book for you Readers. As in our other books, several of us Beings would come forth and we would close the book, so to speak—close that chapter in the book's life. We finish and then the author makes her closing statement by writing an Epilogue.

We have led you through a maze of conflicting information. That is what it looks like when one is speaking about the commingling of different energies in different realities. We have told you of the three realities that were prevalent during the time of the crucifixion. To make it simpler, we could just say that in the fifth dimension, none of that happened, none of it happened. I do not have to reiterate—count them off for you—for by this time, you already know. I will say that the other two realities are confusing. I can well imagine what it must be like for you to try to make sense of this. That is why we have talked about it so much.

With each chapter, we have attempted to explain in a way that perhaps you would understand. This author needed clarification several times, so several of those chapters are because **she** needed to get it. Therefore, do not feel bad, Readers, if you still feel confused; it is only natural. You see, when one's belief systems are so cemented in, there is an energy that forms around that. It is a non-flexible energy. Consequently, what you are doing as you read about the new ideas is that you are actually breaking up a very dense energy that permeates most of your belief systems, having to do with the Biblical scene.

It stands to reason that when a person, probably from birth on up, is repeatedly presented with these different realities, an energy would build and surround him. The energy becomes more and more dense. If you could think of it as carrying around this denser energy, maybe that would make it easier for you to transmute it. How does one transmute a former belief? You transmute that by letting new ideas in!

This author is a senior, and she has found that being in a senior community, many of the seniors are cemented in their particular ways of approaching life—what they believe and what they do not believe. If they firmly believe that the Masters do not come forth and speak to human people except at certain ashrams, but never for the average person, then you are not apt to let a new idea in—especially if it comes by way of channeling. If you do not embrace any words that have come from someone who channels, then you will not let any new ideas in either.

Consequently, it becomes a double whammy. You cannot let anything new in because you do not believe that words from the higher Realms from the Masters are possible for the average person. On the other hand, if you cannot break that energy up, how can you let anything else come in? Therefore, you see it becomes a difficult task to take on. **How does one stay flexible? It must be a conscious choice**. Every time you come to a decision whether to do this or that, ask yourself *am I being flexible? Is there possibly another way of looking at this—another choice—something I might learn if I choose this?* Then try it on for size. Remember our metaphor of using clothes. Try on this new dress or suit for size. Does it fit? Is it too large for you? If it is too large, metaphorically speaking, that could mean the idea may be too overwhelming for you. However, dear Readers, you may never advance your consciousness unless you are willing to make different choices and be flexible—just be flexible! I would say that is probably the main lesson for you—**flexibility.** Now maybe you have not thought of *flexibility* as being a part of making choices. You have it on a more physical level—being flexible whether to go to bed early; or being flexible to drive another direction in your car. However, those are choices. So many people strangle themselves by the fact they cannot be flexible.

Therefore, reading a different book that you may have thought you would never read shows flexibility. You were flexible when you bought the book. One of the biggest hurdles is being flexible with one's spiritual ideas. Are you a Fundamentalist? That is an interesting phenomenon, for they have little flexibility. That mentality spills over into their life. It is always their way and with little flexibility to change their way. When talking about *flexibility,* people do not realize just how broad a band of energy it is that can influence every aspect of their lives.

I was flexible in those Biblical times. I had to be quite flexible. I had to know when to be in a certain place and when to get out. I had to know when to be in a certain country or when to leave. I did have the ability to sweep away the chaff from the wheat kernels, which is the same as saying the lies from the Truth—the inflexibility from the flexibility. I was able to do that.

I believe that humanity's inflexibility stems from parenting, for parents control their children in a mighty way in order to make them conform to their way of thinking. Their way of thinking many times is for the safety of the child. However, as the child grows, the control grows with it. Now there is more fear. There is fear that if the child associates with that person or another person that he or she may get into drugs or into sex, which is always a loaded word in most families. *There must be no sex before you are married.* Consequently, there is a guilt trip laid upon the person as he and she is led by hormones to try out what has been forbidden. Now is this wrong? I cannot make that judgment for you, for there are too many mitigating circumstances.

Was this your pre-birth agreement? Is this purely free will? Are you in defiance of your parents' wishes? Are you being promiscuous and out of control? All of this enters into a decision like that. Thereby, these are choices, Reader; these are choices. As a young person, you also have a choice as to what you wish to believe in your spiritual life. It becomes more difficult for young people to attend church, for the dogma that is taught them grates on them. It is irritating to them in some way that they squirm. They are impatient. They are attending church because it is expected of them. Their parents take them. However, is it for the benefit of the child? Hmmm, again this is a loaded question.

What church are they attending? Is this a church that has a strangle hold on you and projects fear on you, sin on you? All of the things you have heard about may not be true. Are they flexible? Some churches are becoming more flexible. However, the majority of the churches are more afraid of losing parishioners than guiding them with words of wisdom the pastors may have heard from their own Masters—that **I** may have whispered in their minds. If they are deeply connected to God, then maybe God has told them. They become fearful, for if you lose parishioners, you lose money. It is sad for me to see how money controls the churches, for the churches rely on people's giving. Out of this comes the salary for the pastor. If he has a huge church, he has a huge salary. If he loses a thousand people in his church, he loses a chunk of his salary. Would he dare tell people that **Judas did not betray me**? On the other hand, let us back up a bit. Would he dare tell his congregation that Joseph and Mary conceived Yeshua in the natural way? The pastor would have people walk out before the conclusion of his sermon. You see, Readers, flexibility. Those people who would walk out are not letting any new idea come forth. They do not want to change their belief. They are comfortable with it. If they change their belief, it is frightening to them. It rattles them. If you take the very foundation of their spirituality away from them, then they have nowhere to turn. It is like being on an island and having the island submerge in a hurricane. The people are left with nowhere to plant their feet.

That is why we have cautioned this author to be selective for now, as to whom she will sell this book. Are the people ready to hear new ideas? Do they have a New Age mentality? Here is an interesting thought: Many people have studied to become Reverends. Many of the New Age people have Reverend before their names, so that what they say then is more acceptable. However, what is their belief? Are they ready to let go of most of the stories in the Bible? There are very few facts in the Bible. Most is fiction.

I have suggested putting the so-called facts into the category of *Mythology*. Let it rest in historical mythology. Sometimes looking at something from a different perspective like mythology could lessen the blow—could lessen the reverberation that happens when you find out that so much of what you have been told and read in your Bibles is not true. So much of it was distorted by the scribes, for if they did not understand it, they would just project their own ideas—*oh, he must have been saying that.* That is also what happened with the church fathers. They would take out passages with which they did not agree and say, *Humanity will not understand that.* They actually were protecting their own power over humanity.

Do you think that people would pray as they do if they knew the Truth, instead of *Jesus save me; by your blood, Jesus, I am healed; by your crucifixion, Jesus, my sins are washed away*? **That is not Truth**. That is interpretation by church fathers. That is all interpreted to control the masses. **I have told you there was no Last Supper where I took wine and said *this is my blood; drink it and I took bread and said these are my bones; eat it.*** Why would I do that? This was created by the church fathers—what has become Holy Communion. You go to church and are given this tiny glass of grape juice and are given a wafer, and there is the ritual. The real young children only know they are getting juice and a cracker! It means nothing to them, for they do not understand it. Older people in their righteousness believe that this is what I said. Now are they flexible enough to hear me when I say that that never happened? That would be a choice, would it not? That would be a choice whether they could let new information in. You see that is where your flexibility is ruled by the choices you make. Now I am aware, Readers, how different people react. If you need an example, I will say that as we gave this author new information through her mental body that she heard telepathically and recorded, we felt her body react.

Her mind would start questioning. She was able to control her questions and just concentrate on what words she was mentally receiving.

When the author first heard that it was not me on the cross, she did have to pause and think about that for a while. She had to hear it repeatedly. She does not play video games or games on her cell phone. Therefore, she was not familiar on how virtual reality could be. Therefore, she too struggled when I told her that I had created a hologram of myself. That is what humanity saw on the cross. That is a difficult concept. However, she carries a great deal of flexibility and is always willing to try something new, if it is safe to do so and if it is moral of course to do so.

Many of you Readers will have struggled with the information in this book. We made it as simple as we could. We brought forth different Presenters, the Apostles, and they would refute some of the old stories that were written about them. This is your opportunity then to make the choice whether to believe them or not. Now this was not any Tom, Dick, or Harry who was coming forth to speak to the channel, for only the highest Beings are let into her mental body. We have said that anyone must come through me. I stand at the gate of her mental body, and she is greatly protected.

Therefore, when I said that *this is Peter*, it **is** Peter. When I said *this is Judas*, it **is** Judas. When I said *this is Jacob*, this **is** Jacob. What you read in the book as each Presenter came forth was an aspect of that person in that particular time frame thousands of years ago. You know that is not all that unusual when you think in terms that **you** are thousands of years old. **You** have lived many lifetimes. This channel has lived around only fifty-three lifetimes, but she was able to do what she had come to do and then leave. She is a part of the Father and me in energy.

She was Mariam, my sister. She was part of the Holy Family and therefore, part of our Soul group and therefore, part of me— just as you are a part of other soul groups. There are many souls in a group—we will say one thousand and counting. Many Souls are in my group, and I know each one of them intimately and have had lives with them. Therefore, is it not natural then that I came to this author and started writing books with her? Is it not natural then that this was agreed upon before her birth? It is most natural. It is what souls do.

Some people think *some lives are so famous or so high and mighty—what about the person who comes in as a blue-collar worker or as a menial laborer? You never hear about lives like that.* I say to you, dear Readers, this author paid her dues. She was the poorest of the poor urchin in those horrible times in England. Many of you have seen the movie *Oliver* about all the street urchins, thieves, and orphans. She was one of those children in a similar lifetime. She was a peasant woman in Scotland. She and her husband smuggled liquor. She wore homespun skirts and blouses. She has had typical lives of hardship the same as all of you have had. She has had typical lives of grandeur, the same as all of you have had. She has had Biblical lives simply because she is part of my soul group. She also has had lifetimes on other planets and in other Universes. She is old, ancient you could say, on a soul level.

Therefore, Readers, again there is the choice to be flexible in your thinking. In this lifetime, the author had a difficult life. She worked very hard to earn where she is today—a highly-educated, respected, senior woman. She was asked before she was born if she would take on the writing of these books. She agreed wholeheartedly. However, was it easy for her in the beginning? No, it was not, but she has the type of personality that when she starts a task, she finishes it. It may take a tremendous toll on her, but she still finishes it. Those are her choices. She must be flexible every inch of the way. That has become her nature now. She is flexible in her thinking and in her ideas. She questions. She questions the reality that is around her. Readers, you too must question—question your flexibility in the choices that you are making in your life. Are you doing something simply because you have been programmed to do that forever, or can you make a change and try a different way? There are always choices.

Therefore, we are concluding this book for you. There will be a fifth book, after we have let this one sit for a while. We will watch how it has been received. The fifth one will also be controversial, but I think we will let that be a future book you can anticipate. Let us put it that way.

Dearest Readers, thank you for hanging in there and being willing to be flexible and to change your belief systems. It may be a struggle for you, maybe for most of you, but oh, Readers, you will learn so **much** if you can let go. Let go of all the old stuff! Let it go. With that, dear Readers, thank you for the privilege of speaking with you in every chapter. I bless you, **I AM Yeshua-Sananda**.

*All right, dear one, I have done **my** thing. (*Yes, you have, laughingly)*. The next one to come forth for the Closing Statement will be my Mary.*

I am Mary Magdalene. We have finished the book. It has been a great undertaking and a great adventure for all of us. It is hard to believe that we have over two hundred pages of information for you Readers, over one hundred pages of presenting new concepts, new ideas focusing on the realities, and refuting misconceptions about many of us. This book looks to be simple and reads in a simple way. However, if you tallied up all the new ideas put forth, you will find that there are many. Since this is my segment, I will concentrate on myself.

Many people throughout the world channel me. There are many who **think** they channel me. Therefore, Readers, I would caution you to be discerning, for there are various books out there that are not accurate, as I hope you know by now. Some authors say they have a vision and are writing the words they hear, but the words they are writing about me are not true, nor was I part of that vision. Therefore, do not trust every book that you select.

The Ultimate Experience
CLOSING STATEMENTS

That leaves it right open to question whether you can trust this book. I say to you, *yes, you can.* You can trust this book.

Yeshua has blended with his Higher Self, Sananda, and they have orchestrated this book along with the Higher Part of this author. You know when there is an author involved, he or she is involved at all levels. If the person is from the higher dimension, then it is the Higher Self that is involved, as this Soul is. This is a book that will make you think, a book that will trigger various reactions in you, some of which could be incredulous, others could be doubtful, unbelieving. However, it is hoped that you will be flexible, as Yeshua was suggesting. Open your hearts and minds to new ideas. That is such a hurdle for humanity. People become so cemented in—the only word for it—cemented in as the only way of perceiving the world. They are not apt to change.

When your history, the Biblical history, tells the different stories and what was spoken, how does one separate that chaff from the wheat, for we are speaking of thousands of years? That is mythological in nature. That can be mythology. We would rather you would put the information that we have given you in a mythological category than to negate it entirely. **If you cannot hear or read the Truth at this time, then set it in a category in your mind as Mythology**. Just let it rest there. You can also put the various teachings that you have been taught throughout your years on the whole Biblical scene in the mythological category. Let them both be there. Have a file. Those of you who know computers know that they use files. Start a file marked *Mythology.* Occasionally, you can open that file and read it. Maybe by then you can see perhaps where one reality makes more sense than another does. You can sift through them. You can then delete the file. You can delete it and let it go.

Humanity uses its free will to embrace a particular belief. That is human nature. However, people then are reluctant to let a particular idea go into the wastebasket. How many times throughout your life have you changed your beliefs? It can be very simple. What did you believe as a little child? Did you not believe in Santa Claus? With the great wrenching of your emotions, were you not told that he was a fairy tale? That hurt; you felt lied to and felt as if something precious had been taken from you. Therefore, we do know what it will be like for many of you who believe in the Biblical scenes.

You may believe that I was never married to your Lord. You believed that I was a *fallen woman.* There is a great story in the Bible of a woman weeping over the Lord's feet, washing his feet with her tears and drying them with her hair. That is a beautiful story, but not entirely true! Of course, I washed my Lord's feet. He was my husband. I washed them with water and not necessarily with my tears. I dried them with a piece of cloth. My hair was not as long as portrayed. Since it would be warm, many times I bound it up with what you would call a kerchief—a band of cloth that I would wind around my hair and knot. It kept the dust out of it and kept it off my back. Therefore, here is another myth; or I will say another story that you can put in your myth folder.

There is another story where I poured anointing-oil on his head. I do not believe that is true. We did use oil to smooth the sunburned skin. We rubbed it into our arms, hands, and face. It is purported to be expensive oil. I do not believe that is Truth. One of the best oils was olive oil. We were able to purchase the more refined oils that we could use on our body. All those endearing stories, Readers, are in my mind as mythology.

You will find that as you let one of the stories go and put it in your mythology file, it becomes easier to approach the other stories. You will find that you have started making choices and are able to be more flexible with the entire Biblical scene. That is the purpose of this book. As each of the great Presenters came forth and refuted different things that were said about him, he was not coming from ego, although he may have been wounded from the remarks at the time. The purpose was to help you with making a choice whether to believe it or not. It was to help you become more flexible in your thinking.

The Ultimate Experience
CLOSING STATEMENTS

If a Reader has started at the beginning, and we hope you have and read everything from the Dedication to the Preface to the Introductory chapter and forward systematically, you will be led to this Conclusion and will have been given the opportunity to make many choices. Now since this is at the end of the book, we know that some people just jump to the back and read the Conclusion and then they will flip back and read a chapter here and a chapter there. I hope you are not one of those, for you will miss much if you do. There is a flow in this book from one segment to another. They build on each other. They build you to the climax of the crucifixion itself.

I am, as you know, the Twin Flame of Yeshua. We are together many times and we are separated many times—as above, so below. We are not always together in the Heavenlies and were not always together on Earth. Each of us has his/her own calling. After we had achieved bringing in our children and watching them grow, there came a time when we had to separate for a while. Both of us knew how to bi-locate so that we could go to each other, even for just a few minutes sometimes, or longer, and not feel that separation so much. It would be like a sea-faring Captain who comes into port, meets with his family, and then goes out to sea again. You know that he is there and you know that he will return and that you will see him. That is the way it was with us. Our hearts are one. We knew pretty much what the other was doing and feeling. Of course, in our sleep time we also came together. In many ways, it was an endearing life. Many people have hardships in their lifetimes. In reality, ours was no different. We had choices and had to be flexible in our thinking. We had to listen to God and to move on when we were told. This does not happen that much in modern times. It is sad to see that.

How many of you listen to that Higher Part of you, your I AM Presence? How many of you listen to God? When he says *move from that house*, how many of you get the message and move, or do you stay put, using your free will? As the Earth makes her various changes—and they will escalate, for we are seeing it now in your wars, in your weather—there will be more volcanoes and earthquakes yet to start in rapid succession. You will need to listen to your guidance more and more. You need to give yourself private time, even if it is only a half hour each day. Sit by yourself, even if you have to go into a closet—sit by yourself, and listen to your heart's call.

Some people have what they term their *walking meditation.* They walk in peaceful meditation in a peaceful area and that gets them away from the bustle of activity at home. Try to pick a spot where you are not walking along a busy street, for you are merely breathing the gas fumes of the cars that whiz by. Most people can find a sanctuary for a short period. You can go into a library and pick a spot, take a book from the shelf or bring a book, open it, and zone out. Let your Higher Self or God talk to you. Let your guides talk to you. It is so important to create a still space for yourself.

Most people believe, unfortunately, they will not hear God, or hear their guides. They know other people can do it, *but it won't happen to me,* they think. They need to give themselves a chance! They need to pick an area, a park bench, any place, a rowboat, any place for just a short while, so that God can speak to them. He is with you all the time. When I say *God,* I am referring to the Father. He is with you. He is in your heart. Speak to Him, still your mind, and then wait for Him to speak to you. Most likely, it will come as a thought. Be flexible in your thinking. There is that expression, *give it a chance!* How are you going to know if you do not give it a chance? By **it,** I mean to let God or the Masters speak with you.

In this *Closing Statement,* I wish to convey to you Readers how much I appreciate the many prayers you have said in my name—the good thoughts that you have sent me. I feel them. This may seem strange to you, but for those of you who have bought this book, know that my energy is in the book, and I will know **your** feelings from reading it. I will know how you feel about me. Therefore, know how **I** feel about you when I say that we on our side in the Heavenly spheres love you and admire your courageousness for being a part of the changing world at this time. With that, I bless you, Readers. I hope you have enjoyed our words as much as I have enjoyed giving them to you. **I AM Mary Magdalene**.

I AM Mariam. I am feeling somewhat sad today, for I know our book has concluded. I am such a part of this author that I feel her emotions, you see. She always goes through a grieving process when a book is finished. I cannot say that I blame her for that, for she basks in the energies of the Masters when they are speaking with her.

As you have surmised by now, Readers, life had its ups and downs in those Biblical times. We were enacting history, although we did not think of it as such at the time. However, now I can look back at it over two thousand years ago. I see the impact that it had on the people and the world. People are still treasuring the stories. They treasure the stories and their beliefs, even though they are not true.

We are suggesting for those of you that are having a hard time with this material to put it into the category of *Mythology*, as Mary Magdalene suggested. Maybe this will help ease some of the discomfort you may have over the material. Is it not interesting that even though the Biblical stories were not necessarily true, they did carry the energies forth? They were carrying the Masters' energies. They were carrying Yeshua's energy and they were carrying Mary Magdalene's energy, for she has a huge following even to this day. People are more in touch with the Goddess energy and realize that this is what Mary Magdalene was anchoring when she was in France. She anchored it in many of these countries, not just the one. Yeshua was all over the map, we could say, anchoring his energies, releasing the Light codes.

Therefore, what you are feeling today are their energies. You feel that Christ Consciousness even though the stories are not

The Ultimate Experience
CLOSING STATEMENTS

true. Some of you Fundamentalists who I am speaking to may be afraid to touch this work. You put so much credence on the Word. Many times those Words are not accurate, but it is the energy of the Words, you see—the **energy** that permeated the Bible, God the Father's energy, Yeshua's energy, Mary Magdalene's energy, Mother Mary's energy, Judas' energy, Father Joseph's energy, and the Apostles' energies. You see they all were real. They were not holograms, for they were real. Therefore, their energies permeate the world. Moreover, lest you forget, their energies permeate this book, whether the words are true for you or not. Their energy permeates this book.

Put it into the perspective that while the stories might not be true, the beautiful love and peace of the energies of the Christ Consciousness are still with humanity today. Years ago while she was living in Minnesota, this author was given a dream showing the Christ Consciousness increasing on Earth. She saw beautiful shades of pink, yellow, and blue. She felt it deeply, so that when she awoke she was still in that energy. The energy, dear ones still permeates the world.

Since this segment of the book is for concluding statements, I will talk mainly about the book. However, I do wish to say a word on the Middle East wars. The dark energies are rising. It is your prayers that will bring Light to that area and transmute the dark. As you know, when the dark is fighting, things might get worse before they can get better—every moment that you switch your thinking over to the Middle East, say a prayer for it. When you see it in the television news, say a prayer for it. When you read it in the papers, say a prayer for it. It may only be a few words, but it is still a prayer. These mini-prayers do a great deal of help—they are helping.

This book is the longest we have given yet. The fifth book will be even longer. I have just surprised the author about that one. She does not know what it is going to be about and I am not going to tell her (*smile*). It will be even longer. For those of you who anticipate this, the fifth book will be finished probably

192

by next springtime, for it has not been started yet. It probably will not before the first of the New Year. When you think about it, this book was started in mid-June. Then there was mid-July and now it is mid-August and it is finished. We will say our part is finished. The author still has the mopping up to do—the Dedication, Acknowledgments, and Epilogue. It then goes to our dear friend, Heather, who has the joy of proofreading it, for she is the one who puts in or takes out all of the commas, etc.

Dear Readers, we are gratified that you have hung in there! We do hope that you have the flexibility that Yeshua was speaking about to change your beliefs, to change some of your thinking—even if you cannot change it all, do change some of it. Those are choices, you recall. You have choices to be flexible, not only in what you do, but in what you think. Choices are always there. With that, I will conclude. Thank you for reading my words. Know that that lifetime was a grand experience, a grand experience. One could say that I loved and lost (*laughingly*). I loved Yeshua and lost him to Mary Magdalene (*smile*), but then I married my Nathaniel, found love again, and love in my son, Benjamin. It was quite a life. I thank you, Readers for having me be a part of your life for this short period. **I AM Mariam, the sister of Yeshua**.

Good morning, to all of you, **I AM Father Joseph** and I guess you know by now that when I say *Father*, I mean I was the Father of Yeshua ben Joseph. He was the apple of our eyes—Mary's and my eyes. He was such an interesting son (*laughter*). He had a mind that would not quit (*more laughter*). You think you parents have a hard time answering all of the *whys* of your children. You should have had Yeshua (*laughingly*). His questions really made you scratch your heads and think. Sometimes I would even say to him, *Yeshua, let me think about that. Let me think about that.* I would then go about my carpentry work, wax, sand, and think. *What does he mean when he asks that? How can I ever explain that one to him?* I would always find the way. I believe I was being fed the answers by our Father. Our son was deep—a deep thinker.

He also had such a kind nature. He loved everyone so much; he was just kind. I do not think he had a mean bone in his body, which is very unusual, for most people, or I will say the majority of people, have been mean in their lives one time or another. I never saw this in him. That does not mean he could not be fierce in his anger and not stand up for what he thought was correct thinking for some problem. However, I never saw him strike out in anger. He never hit anyone in anger, and he never cursed anyone.

I never once used any of that type of language toward others. However, I admit on occasion I said a curse word, but I never brought the Father's name into it—just a short curse word when something did not go right for me. I think I stuck mostly to *damn* (*smile*). You see we even had that word back then. I never cursed my children and never cursed my wife. When something did not go right in my carpentry, every once in a while I would say *damn, I did not get that quite right*, for I knew I would have to do it all over again, and it would require a great deal of work.

I am giving you a little picture of our family dynamics, you see. Of course, we had our other sons and daughter. Each was a joy to us. We had Mariam, as you know, also. When she first came to us, she reminded me of a baby fawn. Of course, she was not a baby, but around the age of nine or so. However, she had that fawn quality. She had those beautiful, what I call *doe eyes*—deep brown *doe eyes*. She looked fragile, for she was petite. She was quiet and shy. When she hurt, you just wanted to go to her, wrap her in your arms, and protect her.

We soon found that Mariam carried a tremendous inner strength. She looked fragile on the outside, but was very strong on the inside. She also had a wonderful sense of humor after she became more at ease being in the family. Many times, we could hear Mariam and Yeshua laughing it up, usually from the hilltop where they were playing.

The Ultimate Experience
CLOSING STATEMENTS

As time marched on, as you know, between the Sanhedrin and the Roman government our situation changed. Life was no longer peaceful. Then Yeshua went on to his travels. When it was time for me to move on, I traveled to the Himalayas where I studied a bit and then made my transition. My beautiful wife, Mary, found love with another husband, as she ought to have and had more children.

However, our dear Readers, we are at the end of our book. You have been told there will be another book forthcoming. It is doubtful that I will be a player in that book, but then we never know, do we (*smile*)? Therefore, I thank you for the privilege of speaking to you through these pages. We have strived to give you bits of information that you may not have received before—to bring out some of the humanness of our family. The Bible makes so much of some of the stories—most of which are not true—but I wanted to give you a picture of our home life and what it was like. We had a very lovely home. We did spend a great deal of time at Mount Carmel as Essenes, but when we came back from Egypt with the young Yeshua, we soon had our own house. We had a very full life.

When each person dies, he or she has the *life review*. You see, even the Holy Family had its life review. No one is exempt, for how else are we going to learn what we could have done better—learn to see what could have been another choice? You all know by now that there are no accidents. You have not made a wrong choice in that all choices are a learning experience. However, is this experience what you were hoping to accomplish? Therefore, we have our life reviews. Each one is separate. You do not go in as a family and review it in a round-table discussion (*smile*). That is for later if you wish, for you still have your free will. Each of us had his and her review, even Yeshua. I do not know if that surprises you, but no one escapes.

In addition, you get another perspective, for you are able to see the whole picture. *What was it that I was meant to do? Did I do it?* I can say that I did everything I had chosen to do before I was born. I did everything in my pre-birth agreement. I accomplished all—even to the fact that I left and died quite young, for I was supposed to. My work was finished. My work mainly was to bring in your Master. My work was finished. I was not to be a part of that crucifixion fiasco and by now, you know it was not real. However, I did view it from the other side. Many times, I was viewing what they were all doing.

Now, as many of you know, I have traveled down through the ages with different lifetimes. I was Christopher Columbus. Some people in history have strong opinions about him. I have been many people. I was that dashing nobleman, Saint Germain. That was my last lifetime. I still cherish it. I had a grand time. However, I have found that there is a great deal of work to do on the other side, also. I have overshadowed many people on the planet who carry my energy, including this channel. We have a contract and she carries my energy now. Put all of that together and it is interesting to note, Readers that I was Father Joseph and she was Mariam and now I am back as Saint Germain and she is Chako writing a book. I find the intricacies of life patterns and karma woven together very interesting. I am telling you this so that you will know that you too have intricate patterns that weave us all together. We may have connections that you may not have realized yet. There is that saying, *it's a grand old world out there.* Whether you are alive or dead on our side, and I say that we are alive, we are all connected.

I hope that you have enjoyed this book, Readers, for I certainly have enjoyed speaking with you and having my words put on paper. Shall we say for *posterity*, do you think (*smile*)? Do you think this book will last that long? It is an amusing thought. With that, I will step aside and I bless you, **I AM Joseph, the Father of Yeshua ben Joseph**.

Hello once again, my beloved children, **I AM Mother Mary** and I am saying my piece for the last segment of this book. I hope you have stayed with us and that you are reading our words. It was a grand experience, that lifetime. I have not had one since. The others, such as Joseph have come in again, but I have not, for I thought that my energies were better used for **me** to be working throughout the Universe just in Spirit form.

I do come through many channels, as you know. It is better that way, for we wish to get as much of the information out as we can. As you know, each channel has a group of people around him or her that extends out. However, that may not have a further radius, so that then I come through someone else and that energy fans out. Consequently, in that way we are keeping the energy—the *vibrations*, you might say—moving constantly.

I know the information in this book can be heart wrenching for some people. It all depends on how deep your spiritual training from your Sunday school and teachers was for you. However, keep in mind what Yeshua was telling you about the flexibility and choices you could make. The choice for you may feel outrageous and not acceptable. Alternatively, can you let the idea in that *hey, maybe there is some truth here that I need to look at?*

The churches have me in a spiritual cocoon. They see me in a certain way being the ethereal Madonna, love, peace, and healing. I am all of those things, but so are you! So are you, my dear children. I may have had a different experience than you had, and you will have had different experiences than I had. However, that does not make one better over the other, for each experience is precious to that particular soul. It is a learning experience on Earth—the only place where you could get that particular experience—Earth.

If you went to Venus or Sirius, you would have a different experience, but the experiences on Earth are unique to her. Souls ask for these experiences. There are souls literally lined up in order to come to Earth—to have a body provided for them so that they can manifest on Earth. You may think of all the children who have been dying in the Third World countries, and even in your own country of America. However, those souls agreed to those lives and there was a reason for it. I will not go into that, for there are plenty of books where you can read that. The point I am making is that you, too, are a part of God. I am of God, but so are you. I birthed a wonderful son, Yeshua, but you too have birthed wonderful children. Keep all of the Biblical stories in perspective, People. Do not lose your perspective. Do not put us on an unreachable pedestal. I have appeared all over the world, as you know. People see me here and there, but **I assure you I have never appeared on a slice of pizza** *(laughingly)*. I have never! That is very amusing to me. There is a reason for my appearance. **I would never appear on something that was edible!** *(Still laughing)* That is too funny.

Many times, I appear in very heavily-programmed Catholic regions. The Catholics have made a ritual of me. I am almost like an archetype. Is it not interesting that I was a Jew, but the Jews do not go around revering the Mother Mary? I think many times that people forget that I was a Jew. When Christianity was developed and had all of its growing pains and the Catholic Church was formed, they centered their attention on me—the Mother Mary. Consequently, I am known as that throughout the world—the Mother of Jesus. However, I have other names, for I am known in other Universes. In other Universes, being the Mother who had brought in a highly-developed Being is not considered that extraordinary. Therefore, I am not revered there.

On the other hand, Yeshua by his own actions **is known** throughout different Universes and very much admired for the person that he is. However, they do not worship him. **God, the Father ought to be the only one that you worship.** Do not worship the Saints; do not worship the Apostles; **do not worship Yeshua; do not worship me, his Mother.** Many Christians think of Jesus as God. They call him *God.* I believe it has been mentioned in this book that we are all gods, creators, but we are still the Father's children. For **this** world there is only one God, the Father. So many Jews become enflamed when they hear that the name *God* is given to Jesus.

That is where Christianity has so many interpretations. People wanted to believe that he was the Messiah, that he was God. He was not. He was not either one of those! **He is not the Messiah** that the Hebrew awaits and. **He is not God**. There is only one God and that is your Father. He is the one to pray to. You can ask Yeshua to help you in certain conditions, but God answers your prayers. If the prayers are just for you personally, then your I AM Presence is involved, for there is timing involved, you see. Maybe it is not time for you to win the lottery (*smile*). Maybe that is further down the line—the time-line. Jesus always works with God, the Father. Healings only take place when God and your I AM Presence and the Holy Spirit say *now is the time.*

A soul in a body has particular time-lines. Sometimes people must be born into poverty and struggle and learn the lessons around that. Then at another time, they may be given a great deal of money, for that is now in their time-line. They have learned the lesson and may now have more money—God, the Father's abundance.

Therefore, our dear Readers, you are the children of God, and I call you **my** children simply because I feel like the Mother to all of the souls on Earth. We have taken you through a difficult journey—a journey to awaken you and to shift some of those belief systems. Thereby, you can hear the Truth, see the Truth, and know the Truth. We do know that it has not been easy for many of you. However, we also know that many times we need to grow into our wisdom. Knowledge is given to us, but if we do not use it, it does not become a part of our wisdom. It is when we embrace it and acknowledge that *yes that must have been the way it was,* then it becomes part of your Truth and part of your wisdom. With that our dear ones, know that I have enjoyed speaking with you in this book and I shall come again in the next one, for I come wherever I am called. I hear you and I come. I bless you dear children. I bless you.

I AM the Mother Mary, the mother of Yeshua.

The Ultimate Experience
CLOSING STATEMENTS

Greetings to our Readers, **I AM God, your Father** and you have just been hearing from one of my **adult** children who is known throughout this world as Mother Mary. I actually do not call her that, but I will not go into that at this time.

I came in during the Introduction and broke up a myth as to how Yeshua was conceived. The Masters and I thought it best to jump right in and start breaking up some of the stories. This book could be written in several different ways and each time saying what happened in a different way. That is why this channel is not the only one to receive information of this kind. We are speaking to many channels, for each one has his or her own verbiage. Each one has his or her memory library from which we can borrow. Each one, as Mary was saying, has his or her own sphere of people. Therefore, eventually there is someone in every country and every nation in the world who is hearing and will hear the Truth of the Biblical stories.

Now we know that there are great Crusades that visit the Third World countries doing what is termed, *bringing the souls to Jesus.* This may turn some of you off, but let us get that into perspective, also. Think of Yeshua as a gateway. For the first time, they are hearing words other than their paganism, perhaps. There are a great many people still practicing paganism—witches, voodoo. Some of them have a speck of Truth, for much of it is centered around ancient folklore where people worshiped the Underground—the lower forces.

Therefore, in these Christian Crusades, the leaders have great charisma and use their belief in what they call *Jesus* to the utmost. By bringing people to him, they are hearing for the first time a way of living their life, of how they can enter into a relationship with me, their Father. Therefore, Readers, please be careful in your judgements about these great Christian Crusades, for they serve a purpose. They are bringing people out of the dark into the Light. As with anything, one cannot teach the total Truth of such a vast segment of history in one chapter or one lesson. These people from Third Worlds may have never heard of Jesus—may never have heard that there is a spiritual Book that is called the *Bible*. It makes no difference how they get there. It is that they are ready to hear Light and in that way, the Light Codes are entering into them. That is our purpose. They are receiving Light.

If any of you have watched or been at those Crusades, you watched the Holy Spirit come upon those who are near the platform. The pastor waves his hand and everyone falls down, for he is directing the energy of the Holy Spirit. When the Holy Spirit comes upon people, it is changing—life changing—for it is transmuting much that is no longer desirable in the body. It has healed cancers. It has healed drug addicts and they do repent and turn toward Jesus. However, keep in mind he is a gatekeeper and when the people do that, they have taken one step in coming toward Me, back to their Heavenly Home. This is what it is all about. Some of those Crusades reach literally millions of people—millions who are hungry for the Light. If the Light comes through from hearing about Jesus and the stories in the Bible, let it come through that way. It would be similar to listening to stories of mythology. Let it enter that way. This will help transmute the energies that they hold in their body that are no longer desirable. They take that step by the thousands to come to Jesus. However, what they are doing is taking that step to raise their consciousness so that they can rise to another dimension. They are raising their awareness. They will lead a better, cleaner life. They will be kinder and a more giving people, for they have been led to a gateway through Jesus.

Now is Jesus the only way? The Christians think so, but that is only one way, as you know. There are Buddhists. People can go to God the Buddhist way. The Dalai Lama is a very High Being. Many people may not know that the Buddha was **one of Yeshua's lifetimes. He was Buddha.** He carries much enlightenment and peace in his heart from that lifetime.

It is so hard for people who are not familiar with New Age thought to realize that your Jesus had several lifetimes where he brought in different ways of thinking—different paths to enlightenment. Buddhism was one of them. He also was heavily into the religions of India, always the Wayshower, you see. Therefore, I would recommend that you Christians loosen up a bit. Take up studying other religions. Study the Kabala. There is much to learn from those ancient Teachings. Are any of the various religions the absolute Truth? Of course not, for nothing that is brought through human man or woman can be the absolute Truth. **I AM the Truth. I AM the Way**, not anyone else. My sons and daughters are Wayshowers. They stand at gateways and help you pass. Never the less, **I, the Father, am the only Way**.

As you finish reading this book and these various statements, know that in the ultimate end you come Home to Me. That is the title of this book, actually—*The Ultimate Experience, the Many Paths to God.* This Book FOUR is entitled *The Realities of the Crucifixion.* Book FIVE* will again have the main title and whatever We have up Our sleeves will again lead to Me!

I bless you children; I bless you. I am in your heart. Call to Me; pray to Me; talk to Me, for I am always with you.

I AM God, your Father.

(*Book FIVE, Messages from the Heavenly Hosts*, 2007)

SECTION 4—Epilogue

EPILOGUE

Dear Readers, in many ways this book was easier to write than the first three. With those, I was so new to channeling a book that I doubted so much when the various Masters would come to me. I struggled with my certainty that I could do this. Now that this fourth book is finished, I realize that I no longer have those kinds of doubts. I have grown to trust my ability. I was not in fantasy then or now. My connection with Yeshua is a permanent fixture (*smile*).

On the other hand, for this fourth book, the material that the various Masters presented was so unexpected, with such unusual twists and turns that I, also, had to readjust my thinking—*my* beliefs. They just kept hammering away at my *cement block* in order for me to be able to give you their insights on the *Realities of the Crucifixion*. Hence, the repetitions—I think they explained the Realities in every possible way. At last, I can say that *I get it*.

Yeshua, during a private moment, made this comment: *There is nothing further for this book—nothing further. However, we are very happy about how this book has progressed. You have outdone yourself, actually, and have kept so steadily at it. This is what makes the energy of the book flow so nicely, for there are not any disruptions in the transmissions. They go from day to day to day. I can count the days on one hand that either you did not sit for various reasons—to get caught up in the transcribing—or you had appointments. You have done very well, and we are very pleased. Therefore, that can now lead to Book FIVE. Do not be upset if there are a few months' intermission, but most assuredly, you will start channeling again after the first of the year—probably sometime in January 2007.*

You let go of many of your beliefs of what you had read and what you had heard. As each of the Apostles came forth and said that this is not true, you released more of your old beliefs. The biggest hurdle for you, of course, was that there was no crucifixion per se. I can say at this point that you can take every story (in the Bible) and think of it as a fable—every story. I do not care who wrote it, but every story is a myth. The Bible was not put together until years later. Take every story even before and into Genesis—what all the different Prophets had said and their visions—not all of that is entirely true. Therefore, think of the Bible as being mythology. There will be a new spiritual Book, as you have been told, but not in your lifetime.

I have been asked how, as a telepathic, I channel. Do I hear actual voices? No, I do not. I hear their thoughts. Perhaps the best way I can explain this to you is to give you what Yeshua said to me about my channeling, for he describes how the mental body works with the mind in telepathic communication.

When we come to your mental body to give you guidance and information, we draw upon the memory that you carry. I believe it was Saint Germain who told you that he uses your memory like a library. He draws upon the memory from your personal library of your mind. If you do not carry that information for some reason, then the particulars of dates, ages, names, and so forth are not forth coming. A translation takes place when someone channels telepathically. We come close to the mental body, we impress our thoughts, and then your mind like a computer rapidly sorts the material and then comes up with the words. That is why there can be discrepancies, for each person carries a different library, to put it in those terms. Each person has a different library in his or her memory.

I have reread the various chapters over several times during my editing process. Each time I am struck on how much material the Masters have given us. I feel incredibly blessed to be a part of this project. Whether this book is published or not no longer has a hold over me, for I know that those in the Heavenlies are orchestrating the life of the book. I am the instrument and as I mail or hand the manuscript to people, I do so with great joy and no expectations of the book's future. That is in the lap of God.

I now release this book into your hands, Readers, with my blessings.

CHAKO

(You now know that all 9 of my books may be purchased through Trafford 1-888-232-4444 or, Amazon.com. All of the books can be purchased either in soft cover or as an e-book.)

APPENDIX—Reading on Book FOUR

The Ultimate Experience

ZIRANNA-ROWENA'S READING FOR BOOK FOUR—7-01-06

Rowena: It has been an interesting learning time for you, has it not? *Yes, it has, bringing in this new version of Yeshua's life.* First, I will say that both versions are true, but what you are doing is reaching into—because Earth has moved into this new energy—you have moved into this higher dimension. **In those dimensions, the crucifixion did not happen**. Humanity at that time created the crucifixion happening 2000 years ago; it did happen in that lower third level, not even at the third level when you came into this life, but a lower, denser level even. It was out of the second, but humanity at that time created this particular dynamic happening, for they could not move into the realizations that they were reaching toward without that cross experience.

If you look at the fact that everything on Earth is an illusion, it does not make them less real, at one level, so there is room for many different stories to be played out. There always will be some people who never will accept the fact that he did not die on the cross. There is nothing wrong with that, for when they move out of the physical, they will learn another way. The energies that are on the Earth right now are moving into the higher dimensions, as if the old is not true at that level. Therefore, you are right, Anna is right, others are right. She gave a different version from what is in the Bible and all three are right. *Anna, Grandmother of Jesus, by Claire Heartsong (2002).*

In my perception, you are to write your book as you get it. Then when you finish the book, you can always edit and refine it. At that point, you can decide whether to hold it for a while, try to publish it, or publish it and give it to just a few people. I do not think the timing is quite right for that. Your beliefs will determine what to do. **Yeshua really wants you to bring this fifth dimensional version into the printed form**. Whether many people read it or not is not important. What is important is that it gets into the printed form.

Along with that, you are learning many things about self—about trust, which is very important for those who are spiritually focused. You are recognizing that there is more than one way to look at things. They are all right. The other way is just no longer your belief or Truth now. *Rowena equates it to how young children only can see the basic color of something. They do not see the different shades of red.* As the child moves through his schooling, his sense of color expands. When he is near college age, he might see ten different shades of red. In the beginning, none of what the child saw was wrong, but the child only had the eyes and knowledge to see that basic red. There was a time on Earth when people could not see anything beyond the basic colors. Now they can see the finer shades of colors. There are colors one cannot even see physically yet, but they are there. As Evolution advances, they will be able to see the new colors.

This is a very basic way of saying the same thing. It is more complicated with Jesus' life. *Can I simplify it for me by saying that in some way I have gone too much into the Future?* I do not think you have, but in your perception, you may have. You have not gone too much, I do not like that phrase, but you are stretching from this point more into the next dimension than most people, a higher level of the fifth, getting ready to go into the sixth.

You are one of the ones...you know you have prepared for this for many years. *Are you talking in the physical sense, or before I was born?* Well that too, but in this case, I was talking about the physical sense, your life here. You have been preparing for this before you were born for a long, long time. Everything you have done was part of your purpose. **It was important for you to write the first three books so that you could move into this.** If you had tried this before those other books, it would not have worked. (*Laughingly) no, it barely worked with the first one!* **Recognize that each one is a Truth from a certain level of perception, of awareness.** It could look as if you brought those books in first and now they are wrong. That is not true. You brought through what was appropriate in those three books as a way of preparing self to move into this book. Who knows what the next one will be! *I haven't any idea.*

When I get experiences like this, it does rattle my certainty, so I start thinking is this really Yeshua or Mariam? Yes, it is. *(Big sigh of relief.) Thank you for that validation.* However, you are seeing Him at a much different level. I think Ziranna would call him *Sananda* at this level. Just recognize that Yeshua is more than you can ever imagine. **He is so much more than what has ever been portrayed in any book here on Earth.** I will say this that you are not the only person who is bringing this information through. The others also are not bringing it out to the public yet, for the timing is not right.

I bought Suzanne Ward's book written in 2000, and God told her of this. Therefore, she had this in the Matthew Messages, we can say for about ten years. I liken this to science where there is an invention in one area of the world, and another person has invented the same thing on another side of the world. They are all pulling from the Universal Mind. *People who are writing books such as mine, would they be channeling Him also?* They are getting it from different ways. *I was wondering how many people Sananda-Yeshua is giving this information to.* There are a lot; some are willing to accept it and others are not. When you reach the point of evolution that Yeshua and some of the rest of us have...I could channel at least 5000 or more. *Oh my gosh, that gets it into perspective.* We use the strengths and purposes of each individual so that the information may not be framed the same as yours, but the same idea is there.

We really commend you for doing this; we really appreciate that you are willing to do this for us. It will all work out whether you can see that or not. It is all going to work out. *I always figured that when They start something like this, They don't just dump it and race off to another operation. They have a purpose in it or it would not be brought forth.* Some people are getting the information that is not valid because not everyone is clear enough to bring through the accurate information. One of the major learning opportunities is to question whether it is right for me, not for someone else, but for me.

I know there is this phenomenon where it is said that people are just channeling themselves. Well, when I channel Mariam, it sounds an awful lot like me and it **is**. *I do not quite know what to do with that.* It depends on what they mean by channeling themselves. All spiritual channeling comes through your soul. If you are channeling your soul, you are channeling yourself. However, some people think they are channeling soul, but are just channeling from their own personality information. This is where one's discernment needs to come into play.

I think one of the things that will be difficult for me is when people say, and one has already said it, "I'm reading Anna *right now and it is a wonderful book." I agree it is a wonderful book. She is a good writer. However, at that time she was not writing with what I agreed as being Truth.* And you were caught not knowing how to respond. *I do not know how to reply to people.* If someone says, that *Anna* is a beautiful story, agree and say that it is Truth at one level of perception. You are not denying her writing, but you really are not accepting it. At one point you did, but now you are moving on. It is doubtful if you could have moved this fast if you had not read *Anna*. That gave you one structure that you could use to move you into the next level, for her version is different from the Bible's, so there is a progression. She experienced very much in that particular experience, so that is very real to her.

Anna is an entity living back in those Biblical days that still is giving information to Claire Heartsong today. How is that different from Yeshua living back then and Yeshua giving **you** information today? *I had not thought of that in those terms, so I do not know yet. The point I am making is that she still is telling similar stories, which she had said the first time. I feel that she has not changed that.* It is not her purpose to change that. *Also* *where I am coming from is that she is with Finbarr Ross' tour with Margaret Starbird and they are going around to all the different spiritual sites in Europe and each gives her take on what happened. The information is not changing.* It is not supposed to change. They are reaching a certain level of humanity that is not ready for what you are bringing through. Just as you made a step in consciousness, some of them will and others just will stay right where they are—the others will use it as a stepping-stone into a greater understanding. The energy that truly is Anna is greater than what comes through Claire. The real purpose is to shift the perception on how the crucifixion was portrayed in the Bible to this new perception that she brings forth. She does not say there was no crucifixion, but she takes it to another level of understanding, for in her book, He did not die. That is what was important for people to understand, that **His body did not die**. Do you see the progression?

Yes, and that is what I was told in my first books, so I thought, "yehhh, we agree on something here!" That is when I first read her book. Just recognize that each person has a purpose. Each person has a purpose to reach a certain level of evolution within the perception of humanity. That was hers. I do not think that purpose will change for her. There still will be people who need to hear it for as long as she will be in the physical. You can honor her for the Spiritual Being that she is and honor her for being able to bring Anna's energies in so beautifully. You can recognize that it is one level of perception and it does not make it any less true than yours...*and one level of Anna.* Yes, because you bring through one level of Yeshua. Yeshua is much more than that and you know that. *Yes, I only have this teeny bit.* Well, I would not say that. We are not going to measure how that is.

Have I helped you any? *Yes, I will transcribe this and will get it in my head how to answer different people's questions. Now I am wondering what to do with the Wednesday and Monday groups, for I remember during my painting presentation that Bev asked Yeshua about the book* Jesus Lived in India. *Yeshua*

The Ultimate Experience
ZIRANNA-ROWENA'S READING FOR
BOOK FOUR – 7-01-06

replied that he preferred not to comment, because there were theories that could be upsetting to some of the people in the group, because it was not within their time frame to have this new idea come in. Therefore, do I gently tell them about this, or wait until the book is written? I would suggest that you wait and really know that when it is time to tell them, you will just tell them. I would not worry about pushing it. **You** will know as you work from the heart when the time is right to tell everyone. *Heather is my proofreader. Would it be all right to go ahead and have her proofread it or wait?* Wait until the time comes and then ask yourself. Trust that you will know the correct time. I cannot foresee when the timing is right, for there are so many variables that I do not know when the energies are going to shift. *Yeshua will tell me.* Yes, yes He will.

With the Earth moving into the fourth dimension and with all of the Earth changes that will happen, I sense that there is a window of opportunity here to get that information out. Let us have it available in case that window fully opens. We really cannot tell yet how much it is going to open.

I wanted to ask about Judas, for in that reality, Judas betrayed Yeshua, and then he committed suicide. Now I am saying in this reality, did he commit suicide? **No, his suicide in the first reality was not a suicide of despair. It was a suicide of a completion of purpose.** It was easier for him to commit suicide, and again there is some distortion, for he did die. There is no doubt of that, but it was more like a voluntary act of leaving. He thought it was better for him to leave. However, when he left, it was portrayed as suicide. He would not carry that vibration on. *My impression is that he carried that on into the new reality.* Things were different then. I am not supposed to tell you for sure. Yeshua has asked me not to tell you for sure right now. He wants to bring in that information when the timing is right.

It is written that Joseph, the Father of Yeshua, died near his home. In Anna's book, He died in the Himalayas and ascended from there. I have some confusion about that also. It goes back

213

to the different realities. That was not accurate in the Bible. **The scribes did not accept that He went to the Himalayas, so they cannot say He died there when they could not accept that He went there!** Just remember you are looking at different realities and not all are true. *Anna* is not 100% true, the Bible is not 100% true by a long ways, and when you finish yours it may not be 100% true. But you will have brought through the message that they are seeking to bring through whether it is 100% true or not. That is what is important to realize.

If we are seeking to bring forth a particular message, sometimes we distort the information in order to bring the appropriate message through. I bet you have not thought of that. *No, I hadn't. I always thought...* We are doing it for a specific purpose, to follow a specific energy pattern. Sometimes a way will follow a pattern better if we distort it a little bit. What is important for you is to bring it through as it is given to you. Sometimes it is not very accurate, but we have a certain message we wish to bring through. We will bring it through in order to teach or whatever it is for. Therefore, **it is important for you to bring the information through as you are given it**; work through any trust issues that you have about it, but recognize that when it is brought through, you are doing the right thing, for there is a reason for it to come forth like that.

You gave me a new perspective, for that was my old belief system that the Masters always would give me correct and accurate information. Well we do, for what we are seeking to accomplish! It is not always what **you** see as Truth. I do not think you will find anything that distorted, as these two instances I was telling you (*Rowena told of a couple of times while Ziranna was being read that the Masters distorted the information for a learning experience*), but I told you that to show you that sometimes the information is given for whatever we are seeking to accomplish. It can be shifted and changed when you are editing it. With good valued channels, we do not distort the information unless it is within the purpose to do so. We do not expect 100% Truth through any channel because it is important for you to use your energies, your heart focus to help us to understand what will help humanity.

I have heard many times that nothing can be total Truth that is outside of a person. Therefore, the beloved Masters are still outside of me. Well, that is one way to look at it. **I would say Yeshua is very much a part of you. When you speak as Yeshua, it comes from your heart, does it not?** *Yes, it does.* If it comes from your heart, how can it be outside of yourself? You can use the heart focus and that can be outside of yourself, but **when you channel Yeshua, it is from your heart. You are more blended with his energies than you can imagine.** As you some days struggle with physical existence here on Earth, you do not see how that is possible. That is part of living in the physical. It would be nice to say that if you were an ascended Master and created a physical body, that your life would be perfect. It does not work that way, because you are part of the learning experience for Earth, and it is much more complicated than that. You still have the physical stresses on the body from humanity, from the Earth herself. You still have energies that are so prevalent here on Earth, and you have a physical body that does not always understand how to use those energies. Therefore, what do you do? You do the best that you can each day.

I hope I have helped you. I will be happy to help you at any time. *Thank you, Rowena. I needed the validation, since this material is so far out there; I needed the validation that they were giving this to me and they really were giving me this book.* **You are channeling from a high fifth dimensional energy. Truth at that level is much different from the Truth at the third dimension.** *Anna...* is probably at the lower fourth, maybe a little higher, but they are all Truth. That is important to **recognize**

that there is not only one Truth at all levels. At all levels of vibration, there is no one Truth. If there were, there would be no evolution.

Thank you Rowena, it was very helpful.

Rowena (channeled by Ziranna Dix of Sun City, Arizona) is an aspect of the Cosmic Mother and is from the Council of Twelve.

ABOUT THE AUTHOR

Verling CHAKO Priest, PhD was born in Juneau, Alaska, hence her name of Cheechako, shortened to just Chako by her mother, a medical doctor, and her father, an orthodontist. Chako was raised in Napa, CA. She attended the University of California at Berkeley where she met her future husband. Upon their marriage and after his training as a Navy pilot, they settled into the military way of life. They lived twelve years outside of the United States mainland in various places, which included Hawaii, Viet Nam, Australia, and Greece. Little did she know that these exotic lands and peoples were preparing her for her spiritual awakening years hence?

After her husband's retirement from the Navy, they resettled in Napa, California. It was during this time that she returned to school at Berkeley, transferred to Sonoma University where she earned her first two degrees in Psychology. Chako then entered the doctoral program at the Institute of Transpersonal Psychology (ITP) at Menlo Park, CA, which is now Sofia U, located in Palo Alto, CA. She successfully completed that program which consisted of a Master, as well as the doctorate in Transpersonal Psychology. Ten years and four degrees later she was able to pursue her passion for Metaphysical and New Age Thought—her introduction into the realm of the Spiritual Hierarchy and the Ascended Lords and Masters.

In 1988, Dr. Priest moved to Minnetonka, Minnesota. She co-authored a program called *Second Time Around* for those with recurring cancer for Methodist Hospital. She, as a volunteer, also facilitated a grief group for Pathways of Minneapolis and had a private practice.

She studied with a spiritual group in Minnetonka led by Donna Taylor and the Teacher, a group of 5 highly-developed entities channeled by Donna. The group traveled extensively all over the world working with the energy grids of the planet and regaining parts of their energies that were still in sacred areas waiting to be reclaimed by them, the owners. They climbed in and out of the pyramids in Egypt, tromped through the Amazon forest in Venezuela, rode camels at Sinai, and climbed the Mountain, hiked the paths at Qumran, trod the ancient roadways in Petra, Jordan, and walked where the Master Yeshua walked in Israel.

The time came, November 1999, when Chako was guided to move to Arizona—her next phase of growth. This is where she found her beloved Masters, who in reality had always been with her. They were **all** ready for her next phase, bringing several books into the physical—mind-provoking books, telepathically received by her, from these highly-evolved, beautiful, loving Beings. Each book stretches her capabilities, as well as her belief systems. Nevertheless, it is a challenge she gladly embraces.

It is now August 2006. She just has finished writing the fourth book. The Masters are now speaking of the fifth and sixth books. There seems to be no end in sight (*smile*).

Comments:
AZCHAKO@AOL.COM